Trey Nickel Media

I0135072

Wife

Life

Legacy

Dwight E. DeRamus Jr.

Scripture is taken from the New King James Version®
Copyright © 1982 by Thomas Nelson, Used by permission.
All rights reserved.

The Holy Bible, English Standard Version® (ESV®)
Copyright © 2001 by Crossway,
a publishing ministry of Good News Publishers.
All rights reserved.
Published by Trey Nickel Media

Cover design by Cierra Cole Consulting
Photo by Tyson Images
Interior design by Adept Content Solutions

Manufactured in the United States.

ISBN 978-0-9989023-1-9

Contents

Dedication

This book is dedicated to my wife, Monese. Thank you for being a wonderful mother to our sons and the wife I need in my life. You are the epitome of a virtuous woman. Your worth is priceless to this family. Our love grows more each day from the start of our wedding day. Love you forever.

Acknowledgments

First, I would like to give honor to my Lord and Savior Jesus Christ for allowing me to write this book. I believe and know that He is the author and finisher of my faith. There were a few setbacks before the completion of this book. However, any setback gives a great opportunity for a comeback. I thank the Lord who continues to give me grace and mercy so I would be able to complete this endeavor.

Secondly, I want to acknowledge my sons David and Daniel for growing up to be fine, godly men. Thank you both for the inspiration in authoring this book. I pray each of you will find the right wife to continue the lineage. David, thank you for helping me with the title of this book. Daniel, thank you for your support in driving me to finish this project.

Finally, to my late brother Floyd, I thank you for sharing your forty-nine years of life with me. Although you never married or had any children, your experience of living as a single man created some of the content in the book. I will miss your hearty laugh, funny jokes, and the ability to light up the room at any gathering. The weekly talks we shared for the past twenty-six years were priceless.

Love the DeRamus men forever.

Disclaimer

The author makes no representation that the subject of the book represents the entire body of this book. The publisher or the author is not responsible for any person reading or following the information in this book. Neither the publisher nor the author shall be liable to any party for any errors and omissions even if the errors and omissions lead to physical, psychological, emotional, financial, or commercial damages, including, but not limited to, special, incidental, consequential, or other damages. References are provided for informational purposes only and do not constitute an endorsement of any websites or other sources. Readers should be aware that the websites listed in this book may change. Our views and rights are the same: You are responsible for your own choices, actions, and results.

Introduction

Legacy through marriage begins with eternity in mind. God grants favor to successful marriages when choosing the right wife (Proverbs 18:22). One of the most difficult challenges for couples who are preparing for marriage is to come together in one accord. I am not talking about natural matters or sexual intercourse because that is not difficult to do. Animals can mate and produce offspring without thinking. I am referring to the spiritual matters before marriage, where husbands lead and wives support the family vision of leaving a legacy for generations to come beyond their union. Marriage is important to God, but our eternal destination is even more important. What are we preparing for our children when our time on Earth is over?

Wife, Life, and Legacy is my living testimony of choosing the right wife and producing twenty-six years of marriage God's way. The purpose of this book is to discuss several basic principles we should consider when preparing for a marriage that honors God. I am not a licensed marriage counselor or therapist. I am, however, an evolving student of the Bible with matrimonial experience. I do not profess to know all about preparing for marriage (no one else knows all). However, I do know God has revealed that the best plan for marriage is outlined in the Bible. The Bible says God does not call the equipped; He equips the called (Exodus 4:10-11), and we are created to do good works (Ephesians 2:10). Therefore, I am called to produce a book that gives God the glory and impacts the lives of others. I do not put any stock in my life coach certification or any of my master's degrees. The Bible is the only instructional manual that is needed for spiritual growth with scriptural principles to solidify relationships that lead to marriage.

Wife, Life, and Legacy will have us think beyond the material possessions we can leave behind for our loved ones. Such things are perishable and will eventually fade away after time has passed (Isaiah 40:8). Preparing for marriage creates a lifetime of favor or a lifetime of failure based on the choice of a wife. We must also be farsighted and have the vision that we will be someone's ancestors, and how we live our lives will impact our children and children's children (if blessed to have children within the marriage or adopt them). Marriage is not for everyone and not everyone will be married. Although marriage is a common stage in this life for many, it should not the goal in our lives.

Time must be spent more on marriage preparation instead of wedding planning. However, the lost art of patience has filtered down to our decisions of choosing a potential spouse by living with that person. Most of us have the urge to satisfy our sexual needs now and not worry about marriage. It is apparent that couples living together fall into the "test driving" or "try before you buy" syndrome before marriage is even considered. Divorce rates in America are just under 50 percent for both believers and nonbelievers. Our sinful lusts for some of us have produced sexual appetites for men, women, or both.

In *Wife, Life, and Legacy*, we will unpack several aspects of proper preparation for a marriage with the help of the Lord. This is not a wedding-planning book but a marriage preparation book with the Word of God as its foundation. Readers will be touched deeply by this book and guided to understand themselves in their quest for death-lasting marriages. This book will also explain why men and women are equal in relationship to Christ but not equal when it comes to the roles of husband and wife in marriage. Love will be accurately defined, and a comparison between covenant and contractual marriages will be outlined along with expectations of what couples should and should not do in preparation for marriage. The institution of marriage is founded by God. This foundation of marriage helps with the church and government—our building blocks of society, which were both established by Him.

Wife, Life, and Legacy is more of a testimony of how a godly marriage can happen to couples who surrender to God (Proverbs 3:5-6). This book is designed to increase awareness of developing healthy biblical relationships that will lead to lifelong marriages. A good candidate for marriage is someone who has God in front and center of their life. If we are looking for "the one" to marry, we must make sure God is the only one at the head of our lives. We spend too much time seeking a soulmate instead of seeking guidance from the One who is the soul maker. Two are better than one no matter what has already been written or said about the single life. According to Ecclesiastes 4:9-12:

> Two are better than one because they have a good reward for their labor. For if they fall, one will lift up his companion. But woe to him who is alone when he falls, for he has no one to help him up. Again, if two lie down together, they will keep warm; But how can one be warm alone? Though one may be overpowered by another, two can withstand him. And a threefold cord is not quickly broken.

Wife, Life, and Legacy is written for those who not only marry in the Lord but plan to leave a godly legacy for generations to follow. So many people make tragic mistakes in choosing the wrong person to date, marry, or even have children with. Living lives that please God for His glory is the goal. The driving force behind pleasing God in our lives when considering marriage is how spouses love each other and the discipline provided to children through the Word of God. The only legacy that matters—what we pass on to our loved ones—is the belief in Jesus Christ as the Son of the Living God and Savior of the world.

We must remember to love God with all our hearts, our souls, and our minds before any potential relationship that leads to marriage (Matthew 22:37). We cannot be the spouses we were meant to be if there is no preparation in the spiritual growth of a Biblical foundation while walking in integrity. Walking in obedience is difficult, but it is necessary to put aside worldly views and take on kingdom views instead. So many marriages have ended and should never begin because men "fell in love" with her beauty and body and women "fell in love" with income potential and material possessions. The true purpose of marriage is to mirror the intimate spiritual relationship Christ has with the church. Therefore, God must be the center of our marriages.

Wife, Life, and Legacy was chosen as the title because the content in this book closely relates to the Parable of the Wedding Feast in the gospel of Matthew 22:1-14. It serves as perfect parallelism of preparation for marriage to a life partner in this book and the marriage of the King's son to humanity in the parable. Jesus tells the parable of a king who held a wedding feast for his son. The king in the parable represents God the Father, and his son, of course, symbolizes Jesus Christ. Initial invitations were sent out so all on the guest list could make plans to attend. They had to be sent well in advance because traveling to the wedding took a longer period in those days.

The first group that received the invitation may or may not have been honored to receive it. They, however, declined to attend the wedding. The second round of invitations was sent to the first group pleading them to come. The dinner menu served at this wedding was topnotch, with all the finest appetizers, entrees, and desserts available. However, excuses poured in from the invitees because they were too busy with their lives from examining farm property to investigating business deals.

The messengers that sent out invitations were ridiculed, beaten, or killed. This angered the king, prompting him to send out invitations to everyone else in the world no matter who they were. Unfortunately, a certain man was not dressed in proper attire for the ceremony. He had an opportunity to justify himself but was unable to. Therefore, he was bound and cast out of the King's presence into darkness forever. The parable ends this verse in Matthew 22:14," For many are called but few are chosen."

In the parable, the King made no restrictions as to who was invited, and He had to make provisions for proper clothing of righteousness stitched with repentance and salvation. The certain man wanted to come to the feast on his terms in any manner he chose. He was cast into outer darkness. The parable sheds light on the battle of the two wills: God and man. Whether we want to admit it or not, the decisions we make and the actions that follow write the pages of our legacy. God calls to everyone, and we can establish a legacy in the Book of Life when we respond to the call. The calling is on our hearts, and the Lord is being patient for our sake. The chosen are those who respond to the call of repentance and take part in the eternal celebration. Those who are saved enter God's kingdom on His terms. Many of us cast our marriages in outer darkness when we engaged in premarital sex, lived with someone before marriage, or never considered God in the equation in the first place.

Wife, Life, and Legacy explains when we decide to marry how important it is that we live our lives with God. This book is for readers to make use of the information with a biblical foundation and to encourage singles to become better partners with death-lasting marriages. It is understood that we will not meet all the qualifications because we all fall short. However, we must strive to reach the highest levels of each of these qualifications as soon-to-be biblical husbands and wives through the Word of God.

NOTE: This author does not endorse hatred, hurtful comments, or other forms of rejection toward those who choose to live in any way they wish. Free will is the grace God gives all of us, and we can either accept or reject Him as Lord and Savior. Outcomes or consequences are given to both choices, and we will be judged for them (Hebrews 9:27). We are made in the image of God. We have enough of our sins to account for since we have fallen short of His glory (Romans 3:23). We are also commanded to share hard truths with others in love (Ephesians 4:15). At the same time, we use our voices and do not spare any details (Isaiah 58:1). These are principles rooted in the word of God. Living out these principles allows any pending marriage relationship to thrive. However, only God can manifest these principles into promises according to His will.

We must look at relationships leading to marriage as a picture within the picture. The smaller picture shows images of decaying relationships that will most likely lead to failed marriages. The larger picture is the attack on the nuclear family structure. Systems are designed to destroy the family by creating every version of families instead of God's original version. Satan is pulling the strings and doing everything possible to destroy anything and everything God has created since marriage was created by Him in the first place.

God has created mankind with the ability to thrive and enjoy life. We are called to live as unto the Lord, to work as unto Him. We are commanded to love Him and love one another by serving and laying our lives down for one another. Many are called by the Gospel, but few are willing to count the costs for eternal life. Similarly, many are called to be single or married but few have chosen the invitation to do it God's way.

Churches tend to overvalue marriage and undervalue singleness through sermons, conferences, and workshops. Both marriage and singleness are special callings from God. If you are called to marriage, you must seek to serve the Lord with the same passion that you would have if you were a Christian called to singleness. *The call for marriage is making sacrifices, surrendering their lives to the Savior and making Him front and center of the marriage.* Whether we are called to be married or live a life of singleness, we must make God's glory our goal (1Corinthians 10:31).

Wife, Life, and Legacy is for readers making the most of the information with a biblical foundation and encouraging singles to become better partners with long-lasting marriages. It is always best for us to seek and serve the Lord first without any other distractions. Marriage and singleness are both unique gifts and wonderful callings from God. If we desire to be married and not remain single forever, odds are that God has not called us to singleness. God may want us to be single or be married, but we do know He has made a calling on all our lives and wants us to serve and love Him today.

The Epitome of Love

The hallmark of all emotions is love. Modern society's picture of love consists of feelings. Composers, writers, and authors have written about love more than any other topic throughout human history. The entertainment industry has fed us memorable lines from movies and songs that we repeat or sing out often and accept as true. A version of love by the chance meeting of bumping into each other is common in movie networks. We have been programmed to think love in this way is something that we saw or read. Countless couples believe that love will carry the relationship into marriage. Love is exploited by bringing in extra revenue with its heavy advertising on Valentine's Day. We forget the problem is our hearts and that is the heart of the problem, proven by this following verse:

> 9The heart is deceitful above all things, and
> desperately wicked, who can know it?
> (Jeremiah 17:9 NKJV)

By design, we are told over and over to follow our hearts when looking for love. We are often misguided by trends and culture as to what love is. It is not natural for us to love others because we want to love on our terms (Proverbs 21:2). We all want and need love, but no one person can completely fulfill our needs. What gets lost is when love is defined as a meaning of chemistry, feelings, and romance. Expectations are set through looks, income, and performance. This makes our love limited. Sin ruins the right way to love but can only be perfected if Jesus Christ is the foundation of love and accepted as Lord and Savior. Only God can freely give without limitation. His love for us through Jesus Christ can mend the ties man severed in the Garden of Eden.

Human Love

Firsts are some of the most memorable moments in life. Our first day of school, first lost tooth, first time riding a bicycle, or first time with acne. The first of anything only happens once in a lifetime. Most people will remember their first love. We remember their first and last name and where the first kiss happened. We also remember if the relationship turned into a sexual encounter with the date, time, and location (if this happened before marriage). This was the first time we developed strong romantic feelings of attachment and love for another person. First loves captured our hearts with no hidden motives or deceitful intentions. First loves were like a punch we did not see coming.

Human love creates both an upside and a downside. From a human perspective, love is not easily defined or even understood. All of us want to be loved and appreciated in our lives. It is a necessary fulfillment we seek. Being in love is a sentiment that can sustain a relationship for a while and may even bring a degree of happiness. Love is not all about romance and butterflies fluttering in stomachs. It is more than chemistry or tingling feelings for the other person. There will be hard times, trials, and testing of that love. Being in love is one thing, but staying in love is entirely different.

There are upsides to human love. We share an innate longing to experience a special connection with someone. This connection may or may not lead to marriage. Sustainable love can happen when it is focused on the other person while accompanied by kindness, self-control, and other fruits of the spirit (Galatians 5:22-23). Love in a relationship that leads to marriage is God's great design of His divine institution. We must be willing to sacrifice everything for the sake of the other and not expect anything in return. Once a couple reaches the engagement stage of their relationship with a specific wedding date, there must be a shifting of loyalty from family, friends, or career to the person being married. We are reminded in the following verses about what it takes to love:

> 12This is My commandment, that you love one another as I have loved you. 13Greater love has no one than this than to lay down one's life for his friends.
> (John 15:12-13)

There are also downsides to human love. Our limitations are what prevent us from loving anyone fully and completely. In a relationship leading to marriage, no couple agrees 100 percent of the time. This is where conflict is born. We create levels on what we love and how much on a scale. On one side of our love spectrum are people, pets, money, or hobbies. On the other side are sex, drugs, music, and alcohol. We can also love anything dangerous, destructive, or harmful. What makes us happy is part of loving anything that can be destructive for us. This magnifies our limitations in understanding what love is. The only thing that we can do perfectly in this life is sin. Our limitations give us the capacity and the will to love but not consistently and completely. In this life, due to sin, some obstacles make it difficult for us to love others at certain times.

Part of our daily routine is dressing up to start our day and undressing to end our day. After a certain point in time, we take clothes off to clean ourselves and put on more clothes. Too many of us fall in or out of love as we put on or take off our clothes.

Many relationships that continued into marriage have ended (in divorce) because someone "fell in love" with the wrong person. The marriage should have never begun in the first place, but the heart does not see what others can see while in love. There are statements like "We just don't love each other anymore" or "I have fallen out of love with him or her." As time passes, there is this feeling of "falling in love" through performance and attraction. Performance can be time and money spent to get to know the other person. Boundaries are not necessary when the heart wants whatever it wants. No clarity is given as to what type of relationship is occurring and where it is headed. Attraction leads to a desire for physical intimacy through sexual involvement. Sex before marriage is a sin, and it complicates the relationship by clouding judgment, causing us to miss red flags and the true motives of the other person.

We show how we feel when we say, "I love you." These three words are easy to say but oftentimes are just noise with little or no action behind them. This is a typical version of love. Love goes way beyond a big crush or intense liking, which fluctuates according to our moods. This idea of falling in or out of love is similar. We fall in love for a time. When the relationship becomes broken, then we fall out of love and are ready to move on. Even couples outside the United States who are prepared for an arranged marriage recognize that it was not feelings or emotions that brought them together.

Love described in the Bible is a commitment to obeying God's commands, rather than an emotion through human feelings (John 14:15). Falling in love is dependent upon physical attraction, happy circumstances, and emotions. Staying in love is dependent on the Word of God. Love is not something that we fall into but grow into over some time. The term "falling in love" should not be part of a believer's language. Falling is accidental or something that results from carelessness. Because God is love, love is never something that we just stumble into. The world may fall into relationships, but a Christian should never blindly "fall" into anything. What are we feeding love to make it grow? Is it kindness, peace, joy, and forgiveness, or is it pride, strife, anger, and harshness? If it is the latter rather, then the relationship will last for a short period.

God's Love

God's love has no downside. This is possible because His love is perfect with no limitations. This author's attempt to describe the love of God is amateur at best. There are so many books written, songs sung, and programs aired, but we still cannot make a final determination of what love means. No man can calculate or measure the height, width, and depth of his love because our limited understanding makes it impossible for anyone (Isaiah 55:8-9). God's love has nothing to do with us; it is based on His character alone. God loves us not because of what we are but because of who He is according to the following verses,

> "7Beloved, let us love one another: for love is of God, and everyone that loveth is born of God, and knoweth God. 8He that loveth not knoweth not God; for God is love."
> (1 John 4:7-8 KJV)

Love does not live *without* the love of God and keeping His commandments (John 14:15). If we don't love as we are commanded to do, then we are being disobedient. The beginning and ending to the definition of love is God. He created it, and He is it before the existence of this world. Therefore, love is eternal. Love of God is almost unexplainable because it explains His character. Everything else—including love—comes from Him, through Him, and for Him (Romans 11:36). We are created for connection with the Creator. No one can love if they are outside the will of God. Love does not love if God is not part of the equation. God is the only one we should consume who can satisfy our hunger and our thirst to fulfill the void in our lives.

God's love is so absolute because it is pure, perfect, and perpetual, making Him the epitome of love. His attributes are infinite, and the depths of his love are immeasurable (Romans 8:38-39). He is self-sufficient with no outside source of power and needs. The love of God expresses the deep and constant love toward entirely unworthy humans. This holds in times when we are not lovable even to the point of human rejection. This love is the most basic characteristic of God because it is the only virtue that most completely defines what a Christian should be. Whoever is great or least, first or last, young or old, it does not matter because He first loved us in our sinful state (Romans 5:8).

God does not love because He needs love. He loves because love is part of His nature. God is the source of all love that no human heart can contain because it will eventually overflow. He hates workers of iniquity but told us to love our enemies. God hates sinners and He desires to save (2 Peter 3:9). There is no other verse in the entire Bible that explains the full extent of God's sacrificial and unselfish expression of love for humanity with the opportunity to receive salvation than this verse:

> "16For God so loved the world that he gave his only begotten Son, that whosoever believeth in him should not perish, but have everlasting life."
> (John 3:16 NKJV)

When God loves us, He is not sending flowers, buying chocolates, or posting messages. He has made a way by sending His only begotten Son to be born on Earth and die in our place. This is the prime example of giving all He must to show His love for us. We are all sinners worthy of wrath, the grave, judgment, and hell. His love demands total surrender. God's loving offer to us is by faith in Christ. This means forsaking all others. Our will must change to His will. To be part of His family, we must deny ourselves, take up the cross, and follow Him (Matthew 16:24).

God has proven this nature about Himself to humanity throughout the history of mankind. He has maintained a covenantal relationship with humanity since creation. God loves us so much that he first created a covenant with us. He then later created a second covenant with us through Jesus Christ. We remember that God's love did not begin at the cross but was in existence before the world was created. Despite our actions and attitudes toward God, a plan for redemption for us was already set in motion. The Bible tells us about the "Lamb who was slain from the creation of the world" (Revelation 13:8). Jesus did not want to die after sweating drops of blood in the Garden of Gethsemane but was prepared for the cross. He looked at the bitter cup and knew this was the will of the Father and died for all humanity to open the door of opportunity for restoration, which was stolen from us in the Garden of Eden.

Love According to the Bible

In chapters before 1 Corinthians 13, Apostle Paul explained there was a lack of love within the church, which was filled with dysfunction and disorder. A closer look shows the church of Corinth was in turmoil. The church of Corinth was participating in sexual immorality, drunkenness, and in-fighting among its membership. For this book, we will limit our description of love in this section in this chapter to those planning to marry. There is a sharp contrast from the definition of love in the Bible.

Paul wrote to the church of Corinth describing a sacrificial way to love others. This was meant for members of the church to say that the proper use of spiritual gifts must be based on love. There are fourteen characteristics for the definition of love in the following verses:

> [4]Love is patient and kind; love does not envy or boast;
> it is not arrogant [5]or rude. It does not insist on its own
> way; it is not irritable or resentful; [6]it does not rejoice at
> wrongdoing, but rejoices with the truth. [7]Love bears all
> things, believes all things, hopes all things, and endures
> all things. [8]Love never ends…
> (1 Corinthians 13:4-8)

Love Is Patient

We must be ready to serve our potential spouses because we love them and endure everything that comes with marriage. God wants us to come to repentance and does not want for any of us to perish (2 Peter 3:9). People are sometimes disappointed by life's circumstances or poor decisions arising from conflict stemming from selfish behaviors, but they still should continue to love each other. Even if avenging any wrongdoing is justified, love will keep this action from occurring because of grace and mercy. Patience comes from tribulation periods in relationships during the valley seasons (Romans 5:3). This is no different from the love between God and mankind. Part of the essence of love is patience.

Love Is Kind

Potential married couples must extend themselves with acts of care and concern for others while expecting nothing in return. We must show kindness by responding with kind words and acts to those who would mistreat us. Pouring out goodwill and happiness for the other person is a selfless act. Rebuking may be in order at times, and it must be done in open, face-to-face communication between the potential husband and wife (Proverbs 27:5). There should be no fear to correct one's faults. The tone of voice must be gentle, mild, and pleasant. The love of God and the love for one another for God's glory should be the goal.

Love Does Not Envy

When others experience success, we must be happy for others. Potential married couples must build on one another and not tear each other down. Some examples are when people pass examinations for licenses and degrees, others receive promotions or raise in their jobs and new converts come to Christ. We must rejoice in the change of hearts in the lives of the people. Envy generally stems from insecurity, discontent, or dissatisfaction with oneself. It breeds ill will toward others.

Envy is what put Jesus on the cross to be crucified (Matthew 27:18). If we genuinely love someone, we must be happy for the blessings and accomplishments of others as well as have no desire to seek credit for another's accomplishments. We must also not wish ill will or bad outcomes for others because we secretly in our hearts do not want them to have blessings that we believe are rightfully ours. The heart must be guarded against the longing for something or someone that belongs to another (Proverbs 4:23).

Love Does Not Boast

Love corrects the immoderate desire to call attention to oneself. A loving person is not a windbag or braggart. He does not parade himself. Love is willing to work anonymously. It needs no limelight or stage, applause, or recognition; it always stays in the background and keeps everything grounded. Our potential spouses should have others brag on them about the godly life they are living (Proverbs 27:2). This kind of love does not exalt itself over others. It recognizes that our achievements are not based on our abilities or worthiness but on God who gives them.

Love Is Not Arrogant

Love is not prideful, arrogant, or full of itself. This love is not overly self-confident or insubordinate to God and others. It is not characterized by a sense of self-importance or arrogance. A potential married couple should always think about counting the lives of others as more significant than their own (Philippians 2:3-4). When love changes from self-centered to others-centered, this will keep the union together. For potential married couples, we must remember that love for one another within the confines of marriage is pleasing to God, and it gives Him glory. If God is the epitome of love, then Satan is the epitome of pride. Both love and pride have consequences, and their roads of influence lead to an eternal destination. Love and pride cannot be in the same room at the same time. There is no pride in love, and there is no love in pride. The person who loves is humble and imitates the love of Christ.

Love Does Not Behave Rudely

The action of love is not rude. It is respectful of others. We must be careful not to be disgraceful or dishonorable by trying to give others a "piece of our mind "when making some point. Love cares about others, their customs, and their likes and dislikes. Potential married couples respect the concerns of one another even when they are different. They never act dishonorably or disgracefully to another person. Thankfulness is always in order in every situation (1 Thessalonians 5:18).

Love Does Not Insist on Its Own Way

Love does not seek its own way. It is not self-absorbed. Self-centeredness is the reason sin has entered this world. Self-seeking love is a sin and replaces God with self (1 John 2:16). We cannot force anyone to love us. If one member of a potential married couple feels they must give ultimatums on getting married or setting a wedding date, then the ceremony should not happen, and the relationship must end. Forcing people to do something not agreed upon and against their will is not love. We choose to love. God will not force us to love him. He will stand at the door of our hearts and offer the gift of salvation through Jesus Christ, but we have a choice whether to open the door. Godly love puts the good of others before our good. It places God first in our lives, above our ambitions. This love does not insist on getting its own way. Sometimes our love means to let go or stand back and watch others fall even when it is not in the loved one's best interest.

Love Is Not Irritable

Like the characteristic of patience, this kind of love does not rush toward anger when others wrong us. If we want to imitate Christ-like love, then we cannot have a short temper. This love does not hold a selfish concern for one's rights. A small spark of petty arguments can lead to a blaze of rage and conflict in a relationship. The need to retaliate or the need to inflict pain is there. Words in response are keys to either extinguishing or igniting the flames of anger (Proverbs 15:1). Infusion of forgiveness extinguishes anger to make room for love.

Love Is Not Resentful

Love offers forgiveness, even when offenses are repeated many times. Love does not keep track of every wrong thing that people do and hold it against them. A key to preparing for a lifelong marriage is amnesia from past deeds and not recording the number of incidents (Matthew 18:21). Couples will never move forward in the present if they harbor ill feelings from the past. This is not love, and it is not from God. What if God had never forgiven all our sins in our past? Our living is hopeless. We must remember love does not keep a mental record or a journal of others' wrongdoings. Unfortunately, in many relationships, some of us keep a record of wrongs done to us to hold it against the wrongdoer. A major factor of any couple staying together until death parts them is that they must live as two imperfect people willing to forgive each other daily. Without forgiveness, it is impossible to love. The totality of the Christian faith when Jesus died on the cross in the place of all is forgiveness. Forgiving and forgetting are love.

Love Does Not Rejoice at Wrongdoing but Rejoices in the Truth

Love rules out enjoying the downfall of others because of their wrongdoings. Love does not rejoice in evil or even condone sin (1 Corinthians 5). This kind of love seeks to avoid involvement in evil and helps others steer clear of evil too. It rejoices when potential marriage couples want the best for each other and abstain from foolish arguments that can lead to serious matters. We are our brothers' and sisters' keepers. True love and friendship never repeat a person's failures or sins to others.

Love Bears All Things

Love will always expose the sin of others in a safe way that will not bring harm, shame, or damage, but will restore and protect. This verse of love is like a covering. Couples will show love by covering each other's faults and shortcomings (Proverbs 10:12). This love does not condone sin, but it seeks to protect the erring person. Love has others-centered and self-centered benefits. If there are any conflicts or issues that need to be addressed, couples should cover each other's faults in public and confront the issues by agreeing to a resolution in private.

Love Believes All Things

Love gives others the benefit of the doubt, sees the best in others, and trusts in their good intentions. The fallacy of perfection is when we write someone off when they fail to meet our expectations. Our love is meant to imitate the love God has for us since He first loved us (1 John 4:19). Love in a relationship leading to marriage is not suspicious, paranoid, or uncertain. If these feelings exist, then love is not present. Love the flaws as well as the best in someone else to trust them. We love our potential spouses better when we regularly receive the love of God in our lives.

Love Hopes for All Things

Love hopes for the best where others are concerned, knowing God is faithful to complete the work He started in us. This means that God's purpose for His people will be fulfilled. Marriage is truly a shared journey of a life well-lived as a union, hopefully ending in heaven (Colossians 1:4-5). This hope-filled love encourages others to press forward in the faith. God's promises that transcend hope and provide assurance because of His Word are on the line and have been put to the test. Hope will eventually end its route and love will take over and continue its journey into eternity. Hope makes the phone call to God and love keeps the connection active.

Love Endures All Things

Love endures even through the most difficult trials. When love perseveres in the face of adversity, it is fueled by the love of God. It moves forward and goes the distance despite circumstances. There is no quitting when preparing for marriage because we must imitate Christ and love all the way to the end of our lives (John 13:1). Therefore, the "till death do us part" portion of traditional vows is never taken lightly. Perseverance is an area that blinds our minds and consumes our hearts when there is conflict and scurrying for the exit of divorce. We must extend grace and mercy to our spouses because we want grace and mercy extended to us. Remember that God hates divorce.

Love Never Ends

Love is permanent and eternal because it existed before the foundations of the world and God chose us first (Ephesians

1:4). Love exists because God exists. If there is no God, then there is no love. Love is like a circle: without a beginning or an ending. Love does not falter because it is constant and consistent while always existing. Couples' love should never falter from the beginning when they first meet to the ending when death parts them.

Examine the love verses (1 Corinthians 13:4-8): this is the ideal way we all can strive in our relationships leading to marriage and then keep the marriage together. Whether there are good or bad seasons, our finite abilities and resources will run out, and we can only be fortified by an eternal God. What makes these verses so real and so true is that God is the source of real, true, and powerful love. This kind of love grows couples together and lasts until death parts them.

Commandments to Love

Love is considered the highest priority in relationships. To love someone is an act of the will, and emotions come along to support. Love is always best when it is new, pure, and worth waiting for. We can give without love, but we cannot love without giving. Like breathing, eating, and sleeping, love must become a daily habit in our lives. Feelings will fade, romance will falter, and happiness is fleeting, but love is the only virtue that holds relationships that lead to marriage together (Colossians 3:14). When it comes to love, Jesus simplified the ten commandments from the Old Testament into two commandments in the New Testament according to these verses:

> Jesus said to him, "You shall love the Lord your God with all your heart, with all your soul, and with all your mind." This is the first and great commandment. And the second is like it: "You shall love your neighbor as yourself." On these two commandments hang all the Law and the Prophets.
> (Matthew 22:37-40)

We are not asked to love; we are commanded to love God first and others second. If we closely examine the image of the cross, we should know the significance of its vertical and horizontal beams. The vertical beam is planted into the foundation of the Earth and points upwards toward heaven, meaning the love relationship between mankind and God, which is the first of the two greatest commandments. This stands for the first four of the Ten Commandments. The horizontal beam is fixated in the middle of the upper half of the vertical beam and stretches across to the end of the Earth. This represents the love relationship between mankind and mankind, which is the second of the two greatest commandments. This stands for the last six of the Ten Commandments.

Types of Love

Although falling in love is not specifically stated in the Bible, it touches on the different levels of love. The term "falling in love" in this book means the love that leads to marriage. There are four unique forms of love found in the Bible. They are communicated through four Greek words for love, which are *eros*, which is sexual love; *storge*, family love; *philia*, brotherly love; and *agape*, perfect love that only God can give.

Storge is considered affectionate love in families to children and extended family members. This mutual love of protection among family members is important, especially for those who are unable to take care of themselves, like babies and elderly relatives. Storge appears in the Bible, but it is used in compound form along with philia in Romans 12:10.

Eros is named after the mythological Greek god of love, sexual desire, physical attraction, and physical love. This type of love is not specifically mentioned in the Bible, but it is worth mentioning. Eros love is the physical, sensual intimacy between a husband and wife. Sexual intercourse outside of marriage is a sin. Eros expresses sexual, romantic attraction. Lack of self-control will turn desires into deeds or burning with passion (1 Corinthians 7:9). This kind of love is what gets many people, even Christians, into serious trouble. Fornication or adultery with the body it can also lead to adultery of the heart (Matt 5:28). Romance novels, explicit pictures, and sexually suggestive movies like pornography lead to these sexual sins.

The term *philia* means close friendship or brotherly love in Greek. Philadelphia, Pennsylvania, is often referred to as "the city of brotherly love." This is the type of love that David and Jonathan had between them Another example is when Jesus showed love for his friend Lazarus before he raised him from the dead after four days had passed (John 11:33-35). Philia is very unselfish and is like the love that soldiers display while under fire trying to save a fellow soldier who is wounded. It is a cherishing kind of love.

Agape is the highest form of **love,** and it is self-sacrificing and does not change. It is important to know Apostle Paul in 1 Corinthians 13:4-8 is speaking of this form of of love. The purest form of love is mentioned last here to eliminate any confusion with the previous three. Agape defines God's immeasurable, incomparable love for humankind. It describes the love of Jesus Christ for his followers. Love for God is the result of receiving God's perfect agape love. Real love never dies; it is eternal like Christ is the Alpha and the Omega. Feelings and butterflies in the pit of the stomach will fade. Agape is a choice, an act of will. It is the only type of love that can last from wedding day to burial day.

At times our mate disappoints us, betrays us, hurts us with words, or does something we are not willing to forgive. What kind of love is demonstrated here? The trouble is, though we want that person who demonstrates love, we do not always want to be that person. We must give love through forgiveness. Without forgiveness, there is no love (Proverbs 17:9).

Even the disciples did not see a clear picture of what Jesus was teaching about love before His crucifixion. They believed Jesus had come to rule by establishing a new kingdom and overtaking the Roman Empire. However, Jesus had to rebuke Peter as Satan's mouthpiece when he spoke against His death by crucifixion (Matthew 16:23). Jesus also reminded his disciples his purpose was to serve humanity and not to be served (Matthew 20:28). After the crucifixion, the disciples had a better view of love and the costly sacrifice required to follow Him. Like the disciples, it is important to learn to love and think about others more than ourselves. There seems to be a huge contrast between the love that God intends for us to demonstrate and how the world defines it. Lust, unconditional love, and self-love are concepts that appear to be love on the surface, but a closer detailed inspection will show this is not the case.

Lust

One of the aspects of being in love but not yet married is the need to wait. Our eyes and minds are enticed by the pleasures of this world with the message that sexuality is an appetite that needs to be satisfied. These verses remind us of the result in pursuit of our fleshy desires:

> 14But each one is tempted when he is drawn away by his own desires and enticed. 15Then, when desire has conceived, it gives birth to sin; and sin, when it is full-grown, brings forth death.
> (James 1:14-15)

This is true biblically, but most couples have already engaged in sex at this point. In view of the tenth commandment in the Bible, we can lust after other things besides people. Lust is simply when you have an excessive appetite for just about anything. Lust can be an uncontrollable yearning for money, fame, or position. Lust lacks truth, righteousness, and commitment. This is a terrible thing because it is the direct opposite of love by its roots in selfishness. Since this book is about marriage preparation, we will focus on people by defining lust as an appetite or excessive craving to fulfill the fleshy sexual gratification with someone we are not married to.

Lust for someone starts when our look lingers long enough for careful study and observation of the curves and contours of the body. The process of lust starts with the eyes by undressing the person through fantasy. Then our minds sometimes consume us with the uncontrollable yearning for sexual contact. We can think about or fantasize about sexual intercourse with the other person without having any physical contact. Finally, our hearts are aching to yield to the temptation and sin with another person for sexual gratification. Something to remember about lust is that it can turn a no into a yes and a yes into an again. We always fight that internal battle between flesh and spirit (Galatians 5:17),

Unconditional Love

Unconditional love is a dangerous term used in many churches today. The term *unconditional love* is not found in Scripture. This was originated by those who do not believe in God and spoken by many who are supposed to believe in God. Ironically, far from being a Biblical term, it is credited to German psychologist, psychoanalyst, author, and devout atheist Erich Fromm. Preachers preach this to their congregation, therapists teach this to their patients, and professors teach this to their students. When we hear a statement constantly repeated, we are more likely to believe it is true. We must be cognizant not to fall into the temptation of using popular terms in society to feel relevant.

God's love is unconditional according to His grace and mercy, but also conditional in His holiness and sovereignty. Unconditional love involves total acceptance, while conditional love involves discipline; both are motivated by a sincere desire to bring the greatest good to and the best out of the object of love. Conditional love is "earned" based on certain conditions that should be met, while unconditional love is given freely and completely without expecting anything in return. Loving conditionally means to love *if* the object deserves the love, whereas loving unconditionally means to love *despite* the object being unworthy of love.

God loves, but this does not mean that He loves everything. We often overlook God's justifiable wrath. We tend to forget the latter part of John 3:16: *"that whoever believes in him should not perish but have everlasting life."* If He loved everybody in the whole world without the redemption of sins, then the whole world would be saved. This is a license to sin by doing whatever we want and believing whatever we think. There would be nothing unsaved people need to do to be saved and nothing for saved people needing forgiveness of sins—after all, God loves us no matter what. It is a waste of time talking about hell and judgment since everyone will go to heaven

> "As the Father loved Me, I also have loved you; abide in My love. If you keep My commandments, you will abide in My love, just as I have kept My Father's commandments and abide in His love."
> (John 15:9-10 NKJV)

Notice in John 15:9 that God's love is a condition set by keeping the commandments. God's love is conditional through our acts of obedience in the Ten Commandments (Exodus 20:6). Then why does He call us to repent, to come to the cross, or to come to Christ? Conditional love sets limits on the sin it will allow. God's love is conditional in His grace and mercy. He sends grace to the just and unjust and allows turning to Him when we wake up and when we lie down (Matthew 5:45). God does not only love; He is Holy. God's holiness creates judgment through discipline. God placed an absolute condition to which He requires obedience (John 14:15).

Self-Love

Confusion is common when we mix our definition of love with the Bible's definition because mankind's love is flawed. Whenever God creates mankind deviates. Our definition of love is skewed because of movies watched or music listened to or even books read (Bible not included). It is impossible to truly define what love is if God is not part of the definition since the concept was created by Him in the first place (Romans 2:5). We even include the concept of self-love or self-esteem into the equation of what we believe love is.

The popular cry for self-love is the first listed symptom of the perilous times of the last days (2 Timothy 3:1-5). We should see ourselves as "worthless." The Bible teaches that we are created in the image of God and our value is so worthy that He knows the numbers on our heads (see Luke 12:7). We must value others by showing love for them without hypocrisy (Romans 12:9-10). Loving others requires humility and giving preference to one another with a conscious effort to put others' interests first. Anything less than this is selfish and vain and falls short of the standard of Christ.

Self-love and unconditional love are byproducts of humanism. Unconditional love is wrong and profane. Humanism is a philosophical belief system that emphasizes human self-fulfillment without the need of a divine supernatural or spiritual entity.

Conclusion

Expressing our love for God is shown when we express love for one another. There is action behind this word that must be shown. It is very much like how faith is accompanied by works;

If we have the first the second will come automatically. This is the full use of the two greatest commandments: love God and love others. When we love God first, loving others will come naturally. For us to receive unconditional love from God some conditions must be met. God's love is conditional by which He requires all to accept His Son as Lord and Savior and repent of sins to receive His love. God's love is the only love that leads us from the wedding day to the burial day. It will overcome strife, malice, jealousy, envy, contempt, and any other emotions that will divide relationships with other people. We must choose to love every day.

We must thank the Lord for the undeserved love He so freely gives to anyone who will ask. The ability for us to love freely without any expectation of something in return could not be done with God's help. Conforming to the image of Christ requires us to love like Him when we show love to friends or enemies. We must do everything for the glory of God, and this includes love (1 Corinthians 10:31). He has shown us the perfect example of love through the life, death, and resurrection of Jesus. God is love because without love there is no mercy, grace, longsuffering, and forgiveness. He is and will always be the epitome of love.

Building Boaz

Our world can be compared to a chessboard. Chess is one of the oldest and purest games ever invented. A chess game is a version of everyday life that is spread on a checkerboard of 64 squares with 32 pieces. Of the 32 pieces, 16 of them are light-colored and 16 are dark-colored on opposing sides of the board in two rows of eight. Our relationship with God determines whether we are light-colored or dark-colored pieces. There are various pieces on the board—pawns, rooks, knights, bishops, queens, and kings. At the start of the game on both sides of the board, the queen is at the king's side. She is the most powerful piece, but the king is the most important one. The game can be won without the queen, but this is not possible without the king.

The goal in chess is to threaten the king by forcing him to move from an endangered position to safe position—called "check"—until the king is endangered and has no safe space to move to—"checkmate." Once the king can no longer be protected from danger, the game is over. The game hinges on whether the king is upright or fallen. Forethought and strategic planning make the difference between victory and defeat. The skill of each move depends upon the hand of the given player. The farther away from Him we move, the farther away moves His hand of protection (Matthew 23:37-39).

Like moving pieces on a chessboard, consider the intertwining of the lives of Ruth and Boaz. Their story in the Bible began as a family business transaction when the laws and customs of Israelites were strictly followed. Boaz followed the laws regarding kinsman-redeemer, meaning to act on behalf of a relative who is in trouble or need by rescuing the person or property to restore. Boaz was described as a worthy man who was a relative of Ruth's mother-in-law Naomi (Ruth 2:1). The story then changed from a business transaction into a love story. Ruth's beauty along with her matching character caught the attention of Boaz. They eventually married and had a son, Obed, who was the grandfather of King David. This lineage eventually leads to the birth of Jesus Christ (Matthew 1:5-16).

Like all mankind, Boaz inherited his sin from Adam. God's original design for the world was perfect after six days of creation. The man was first to be created. In Adam, there was no sin. He was placed in the Garden of Eden to tend to it and keep it tidy for God. This world was perfect with no crime, sickness, pain, or wickedness. Food was plentiful with no threat of a shortage of anything. The sun was always shining with the temperature at a comfortable level. This place could be described as a slice of heaven placed on Earth. God was present as a best friend with an opportunity to love forever.

God granted leadership to Adam before the Fall in Genesis chapter 3. Adam's leadership before Eve's existence is often ignored or dismissed. The second chapter of Genesis is the recap of the first chapter with more detailed information on the history of creation. God presented the animals to Adam to see what he would call them. Adam was given dominion to name all the creatures of the air, land, and sea. Evidence of leadership was shown after every living creature was named. There is no dispute with these clear truths from the Bible. The woman was made from the man, after the man, and for the man. She was also named by the man twice and was brought by God to the man.

Satan knew *all this*, which is why he disrupted the leadership by going to Eve instead of Adam. As a result of Adam's poor leadership, sin and death came into existence in the following verses:

> [12]Therefore, just as through one man sin entered the world, and death through sin, and thus death spread to all men because all sinned [13](For until the law sin was in the world, but sin is not imputed when there is no law. [14]Nevertheless death reigned from Adam to Moses, even over those who had not sinned according to the likeness of the transgression of Adam, who is a type of Him who was to come. [15]But the free gift is not like the offense. For if by the one man's offense many died, much more the grace of God and the gift by the grace of the one Man, Jesus Christ, abounded to many.
> (Romans 5:12-15 NKJV)

Adam was responsible for the Fall, which is why God spoke to him *first* (Genesis 3:9). According to 1 Corinthians 15:22, death was passed down to all mankind due to Adam's sin. Eve was deceived, but Adam disobeyed (2 Timothy 2:14). He was a weak leader. Man's sentence from God changed the concept of work from light duty to heavy lifting, and his lifespan was also changed from a perfect life to one ending in death (Genesis 3:17).

Identity Crisis

The confusion within stages of growth and the maturation process in the lives of people are part of what is called an "identity crisis." For centuries men have been providers of defense, security, shelter, food, and the necessary means for life with women. The Fall created an identity crisis when Adam and Eve decided it was better to act on the fear of missing out or becoming someone else under the influence of Satan

(Genesis 3:16). Now society has been experimenting with what it means to be male and female through extreme self-expression and independence when it comes to gender and roles. This experimentation is largely influenced by what images are shown by the media.

Media has a tremendous influence on how society interprets what gender is and the roles within each of them. When it comes to men, the media injects subtle information with words and images that reduce men to the simplest form of manhood. This doctrine is usually transmitted across the mediums of television, radio, movies, and advertising of all sorts. Men are often portrayed as foolish, bumbling idiots, or even childish without a clue about being adults while women hold families together by their strength and wisdom. In addition, men are considered aggressive, sex-crazed maniacs incapable of controlling their anger. The job of the media is to control the information by devising the situation, creating a storyline, and making it sound believable, which influences our hearts and minds.

The decline of true manhood is real. Two-parent married households are no longer the norm, with men not fulfilling their God-given role as leaders. Less than half of families consist of couples who are married. They are either cohabitating or single parenting. Husbands and fathers are substituted for governmental assistance and a live-in boyfriend or girlfriend. The world has diminished the need for a man in a family because he is being systematically replaced from his position as the head. Boys being unprepared for their roles as husbands and fathers has had devastating effects on this generation and the generations to come. Manhood is under a series of Satanic attacks through fatherlessness, school performance, and extended adolescence.

To begin with, fatherlessness and a lack of father figures contribute to the identity crisis in boys. Nationallty, almost half of children born today come from unwed parents. Even among those children born to married couples, about half of them will see their parents divorce by the age of 18. Without fathers, boys will not receive the modeling of manhood and answers to questions about male identity, responsibility, and roles. They will miss out on invaluable "man-to-man" talks. Topics from these talks may include grooming, money management, sex, and work ethic. Almost any adult male who was reared by a father remembers these talks, and most would admit that times like these made a significant impression on their lives. This is intricately connected with missing fathers because they are the primary male influence in a young man's life.

Boys must be trained to see themselves as future husbands and fathers. They must be taught what to look for in a godly wife and how to fulfill all the responsibilities that Scripture teaches about the role of husband and father. Without fathers present, boys become less successful as future husbands and fathers and are made into weaker and less masculine males. Even some images of Jesus Christ are often *falsely portrayed* as a white, long-haired, hippie, effeminate male.

Secondly, modern education is increasingly sacrificing the male gender on the altar in the name of equality. Since the beginning of the twenty-first century, the feminization of our schools and other learning organizations has pushed girls to increasing academic achievement. Girls are outperforming boys with higher grades and graduation rates on all school levels, and 80 percent of teachers are women. Boys, on the other hand, have more detentions, suspensions, expulsions, and placement in special education. Less than 20 percent of teachers are men.

Boys' academic and behavioral progress would be greatly impacted if they saw more male teachers they could look up to since almost half overall do not have fathers in the home. However, masculine traits such as leadership and competitiveness are not valued in schools. Instead, schools value qualities that are associated with femininity such as cooperative learning and inclusiveness. A systematic reconfiguration of masculinity as some deemed toxic behaviors is the goal. When boys' competitive nature and physical play are limited in a school setting, it is easy for boys to find comfort in video games to quench that thirst for competition and physical play.

Lastly, extended male adolescence is perpetual boyhood on the part of many males. The feminization of school systems helped to push some boys into video gaming. Boys, young adults, and even grown men spend inordinate amounts of time playing video games and consuming media. Video game addiction is about four times more common among boys than girls. The average American boy spends thirteen hours a week absorbed in video games, compared to five hours for the average girl. Contrary to popular opinion, men are not less emotional than women; they process them differently and at their own pace. They show emotional strength when their ears and hearts are opened for intimacy by listening to women and connecting through communication. Suppressing the willingness to have normal face-to-face interactions makes them socially awkward and isolated. This directly impacts real-world relationships, education, and employment. The lack of these skills will affect a man's relations with his wife, children, peers, colleagues, and others. Some of the unintended consequences of excessive gaming and media consumption are that many become disconnected from reality. From the very beginning, we were created as social beings with one another. We must not not retreat toward isolation. The following verse reminds men to grow up and not grow old:

> When I was a child, I spoke as a child,
> I understood as a child, I thought as a child; but
> when I became a man, I put away childish things.
> (1 Corinthians 13:11 NKJV)

Satan has been attacking gender, gender roles, and especially masculinity with a vengeance since the beginning of time when he ignored Adam and went to Eve (Genesis 3). The nuclear family is constantly under attack because the man is established as the head (1 Corinthians 11:3). Once fathers are removed from the home, then it is open season on the family. Schools will do the most teaching; social media will do the most outreaching; and television programs will do the most preaching as to what it is to be a man.

Satan wants to destroy manhood by perverting its meaning and position. This ambush is geared toward all families in general and black families in particular. These vicious and subtle attacks on manhood are essentially aimed at God. They are designed to confuse people to the point where they cannot have the right relationship with Heavenly Father. God made men and women unique and distinct for a reason. Our culture comes up with damnable doctrine as to what it is to be a man.

Call to Biblical Manhood

Manhood has never been under more attack than at this point in history. The world is increasingly confused about matters as basic as what it means to be male. Few people understand what true manhood is as God defines it. Christians are called to frame our arguments in distinctively biblical terms. Biblical manhood can be boiled down into three areas in this order:

1.   A master to answer
2.   A mission with a vision
3.   A mate to cultivate

When choosing a Master to answer, a man must choose God first and foremost in his life above anyone and anything else. This is by far the most important point. Since true biblical manhood is defined as who God wants us to be, how can any man who is supposed to be in authority do so if he refuses to submit under the authority of Christ? Even Christ was under the authority of the Father (1 Corinthians 11:3). These following verses set the tone on the clear difference between men and males in the eyes of God:

> ³⁰So I sought for a man among them who would make a wall and stand in the gap before Me on behalf of the land, that I should not destroy it; but I found no one.
> (Ezekiel 22:30 NKJV)

This verse is like the popular US Marines slogan: God is looking for a few good men among the males present. Every man is a male, but not every male is a man—the type of man whose walk with God is measured by Scripture (Proverbs 10:9). He obeys the scriptures to love all people, even his enemies. He also respects the authorities in his life and the laws of the land. The type of character required is showing good judgment at home, at work, and in the community. Character needs to be exercised in all areas of life no matter how great or small they may be.

When choosing a mission with a vision, a man must be able to define the necessary work to be done and the intended direction God has for his life. There are specific talents or gifts given to every man. Regardless of the gifts, a clear direction must be identified with specific timeframes on how the work is to be done and why it must be done. The lens he sees through is not natural but spiritual. He relies on God, knowing he cannot fulfill his mission without His guidance according to this verse:

> ¹⁸Where there is no vision, the people perish: but he that keepeth the law, happy is he.
> (Proverbs 29:18 KJV)

A vision is a revelation from God that He will take care of the details of the mission through His will (James 4:13-15). Perishing is dying from the ignorant reasoning from our minds apart from the Word of God. It is important to know once the purpose is known, a man can focus on the mission if he does not chase after earthly pleasures during his singleness stage. Chasing the pleasures of this world over the purpose not only blinds his vision but weakens his manhood. The only path to achieve the work in the mission is the straight and narrow way without distractions (Matthew 7:13-14). If we walk by sight and not by faith, we cannot see the big picture from God's perspective. Eternity is in the rearview mirror because it is always closer than it appears.

When choosing a mate to cultivate, a man must prepare steps in aiming toward marriage and fatherhood. Men who wish to marry at some point during their lifetime must become husband material before becoming a husband. God said it was not good for a man to be alone. God sometimes selects certain men not to marry but to fulfill a purpose for His Kingdom in the act of lifelong service to Him according to this verse:

> 8He has shown you, O man, what is good;
> And what does the Lord require of you
> But to do justly, to love mercy,
> And to walk humbly with your God?
> (Micah 6:8 NKJV)

A truly Biblical man is called to fulfill his role as husband and father. The cultivation process is to exercise spiritual maturity within himself with help from the Holy Spirit while building a life with his family in a way that will honor God. In preparation for being a husband and father, a man is charged to lead the family. It is given by God to men, and they must live it out biblically rather than perverting it and redefining it in worldly selfish terms. These are keys to earning the respect and confidence of a wife.

Wife Selection

Each year in all professional sports, athletes as individuals or teams compete to win a championship as the crowning achievement of the season. Athletes are crowned to honor sporting achievements with championship rings and trophies. A crown is a grand piece of jewelry, and a virtuous woman is a crown to her husband (Proverbs 12:4). Based on the choice of a wife, men will either wear crowns with gold and jewelry or a crown of thorns. Wives can give husbands a lifetime of favor or a lifetime of failure.

When selecting a wife, a perfect woman is not real, and a real woman is not perfect. A good wife is one of life's greatest blessings, but a bad wife is one of its greatest frustrations. Men become very vulnerable to the tricks of Satan when a man uses beauty and favor alone when selecting a woman to marry (Proverbs 31:30). A beautiful body with a pretty face and her willingness to please *before* the wedding are not enough when selecting a wife. Her true character *after* the wedding day will determine if the marriage will be a happy or horrible one. The beauty looked at only on the outside is for fools only, but real men examine the conduct that reveals the heart. The right kind of woman will make a man feel great. This verse shows the importance of selecting a wife of godly character:

> He who finds a wife finds a good thing,
> And obtains favor from the Lord.
> (Proverbs 18:22)

The Bible is clear and men, in general, know we are the ones who search for wives and offer marriage. A virtuous woman is a good thing—despite certain areas within the culture where some women are proposing to some men. The essence of a man's legacy for his family will hinge on two things: his relationship with God and the wife he has chosen. His relationship with God tells how well he loves his wife.

Remember, love is not something we fall into; it is what we grow into over some time. Men will not always love and lead perfectly their wives, just like women won't always respect and submit to their husbands. Unrealistic expectations can show an absence of grace. Sometimes grace should be extended through forgiveness because knowing what things should be can make us forget what we are at that moment in our lives (Colossians 3:13).

So, what are some examples of how a woman feels loved by her husband? These are common expectations that most women want from the men in their lives. First and foremost are safety and security. This is reassurance that she is loved and cared for, even in conflict. Second, there must be an understanding that her feelings about a problem are important to her. Take the time to listen to her talking them out with attentiveness. Third, quality time is extremely important, and vacations do not count. Whether it's scheduling date night or planning daily interactions with conversations, it is important to be consistent. Lastly, compliment her often and let her know she is beautiful. This is air inside a man's lungs that helps him to breathe.

When a wife feels loved, it's easier for her to give the support and respect that a husband needs. A wife is either a crown to her husband or rottenness in his bones (Proverbs 12:4). A wife can greatly improve a marriage, family, and lineage into future generations. She can also destroy and ruin the family name from how she raises her children and interacts with her husband. In the end, God will hold the success or failure of a marriage on the husband based on his choice of a wife.

Roles of a Biblical Husband

Today, the office of the husband in many families has been reversed. These men must exhibit the attitude of a servant to fulfill these roles properly. The Word is the only exact and reliable source for instruction. Every man who desires to be married is given greater responsibility as the position of the husband from these verses:

> ^{25}Husbands, love your wives, just as Christ also loved the church and gave Himself for her, ^{26}that He might sanctify and cleanse her with the washing of water by the word, ^{27}that He might present her to Himself a glorious church, not having spot or wrinkle or any such thing, but that she should be holy and without blemish. ^{28}So husbands ought to love their own wives as their own bodies; he who loves his wife loves himself. ^{29}For no one ever hated his own flesh but nourishes and cherishes it, just as the Lord does the church.
> (Ephesians 5:25-29 NKJV).

God's will for every potential husband is sacrificially loving, serving, and leading his family. This is not saying that husbands will not need love and wives will not need respect. Husbands will grow into the marriage better with respect, and wives will grow into the marriage better with love. Love and respect are a package deal since one does not exist without the other. Unfortunately, sin has corrupted both the loving headship of the husband and the willing submission of the wife. And so, the perfect love found in the Garden of Eden is replaced by the battle of the sexes. When it comes to the preparation for marriage, if there is no respect for husbands and love for wives, then the marriage will certainly die.

To love their wives and children, husbands must sacrifice needs and willingly put themselves on the cross daily. Husbands are to be willing to give their lives for their wives and children sacrificially. This is the kind of love that is required. Agape love begins on the wedding day and ends on the burial day. We need godly men to lead both physically and spiritually. The first two tenets, provide and protect, are what any man or animal can do. The last two tenets, priests and prophets, are what men of God are required to do. Men must return to their responsibilities in the home as family providers, protectors, priests, and prophets.

Provider

As a provider, it is a husband's responsibility to lead his wife and provide for the basic needs of his family. This may include the disciplining of children, working extra hours at work, or repairing things around the house. A call for responsibility to families from the Word of God was given to husbands' role in the home that must be modeled and passed on to the next generation. Men were created to meet all the demands of providing for the family in this life according to this verse:

> 8But if anyone does not provide for his own, and especially for those of his household, he has denied the faith and is worse than an unbeliever.
> (1 Timothy 5:8 NKJV)

Headship involves sacrificial love through responsibility, but it also implies leadership in making decisions. Husbands are not dictators; they should not demand, they should not rule over their wives. Wives can disagree with their husbands, but wives are to respect their husbands even when expressing disagreements (Ephesians 5:24). Instead, husbands should influence their wives and families by biblical teaching. Even if there is a perception the wife is more qualified, smarter, and more spiritual, the husband is expected to take the reins and lead. Being in charge and being in control are not the same thing. Control is nothing more than fear and insecurity. Control freaks fear being out of control themselves. Wives and children must not be controlled but loved or the prayers of husbands can be hindered (1 Peter 3:5).

Protector

As a protector, a husband must be ready to put his physical strength on the line to protect his wife and children and to fulfill his God-assigned tasks. He will protect everyone under his care, even being willing to give his own life (John 15:13) A wife and children are to be protected from internal forces and external forces as well. Protecting from worldly influence inside the home from all types of media means monitoring online activities, cell phones, videos, and television programs. Family members and friends must be protected from outside forces. Temptation from others who may cause a romantic relationship is also something to consider. Sex outside the confines of marriage is sinful and has serious consequences. The protector treats his wife in an understanding way, being kind, gentle, and caring of her according to this verse:

> ⁷Husbands, likewise, dwell with them with understanding, giving honor to the wife, as to the weaker vessel, and as being heirs together of the grace of life, that your prayers may not be hindered.
> (1 Peter 3:7)

A young man ought to be physically strong, but above all else, a young man must be *spiritually* strong. It is more than responsibility. This is sacrificial accountability, which shows actionable decisions in loving our wives by enhancing respect for them at the same time. Christ already set the example as the bridegroom and did that for the church. What is honorable and worthy of admiration is the man with self-mastery, who refrains from being entrapped by such sins. We yearn for a man with self-control, temperance, and strong moral character. Christ's example for men today is to not be driven by urges, what feels good, or what is convenient. This world needs men who govern themselves by the same moral code that Jesus had.

Priest

As a priest, a man is a spiritual leader in the home. Find ways to point your wife to Christ by always praying for her and with her. The heart must be right before prayer because God sees the mind and motives (Jeremiah 17:10). A man's connection to his family depends on their connection to God through Jesus Christ. His spiritual relationship with the Lord is essential to the success of their marriage and family. They are the mediators who can come before God on behalf of wives and children through prayer. The role of a priest is to go before his family on behalf of God and go before God on behalf of his family according to these verses:

> Seeing then that we have a great High Priest who has passed through the heavens, Jesus the Son of God, let us hold fast our confession. For we do not have a High Priest who cannot sympathize with our weaknesses but was in all points tempted as we are, yet without sin." [16]Let us, therefore, come boldly to the throne of grace, that we may obtain mercy and find grace to help in time of need.
> (Hebrews 4:14-16 NKJV)

Prayer is for God's hedge of protection covering your home and wife, you, and your family to prevent attacks from the enemy (Job 1:10). This is prayer on behalf of our wife and children, friends, and extended family members as well as for their needs and concerns of others both spoken and unspoken. Outside the home, after general prayer for traveling grace, pray for employers and employees, government leaders, local community leaders, and church leaders as they make decisions that affect everyone collectively. A husband in this role must strive to live a life of complete holiness and guidance from the Holy Spirit to use specific prayers when making decisions.

Prophet

A prophet was someone who had heard something from God. God had spoken His Word to him and revealed His truth to him. A prophet commits to listen to God and then share what God is speaking to him with others. Husbands must adjust

their daily routines to create opportunities to hear God's voice.
God speaks His word through dreams, wives, and other people.
When God is speaking, it is never in disagreement with the
Bible. There is a warning to consider when there are unrepentant
sins like secret addictions (1 John 3:8-9) or mistreatment of the
family (1 Peter 3:7):

> [11]Put on the whole armor of God, that you may be
> able to stand against the wiles of the devil. [12]For we
> do not wrestle against flesh and blood, but against
> principalities, against powers, against the rulers of
> the darkness of this age, against spiritual hosts of
> wickedness in the heavenly places. [13]Therefore take
> up the whole armor of God, that you may be able to
> withstand in the evil day, and having done all, to stand.
> (Ephesians 6:11-13)

There should be some biblical knowledge that leaves man
equipped and prepared for spiritual warfare as leader of his
family. It would be difficult for a Christian wife to respect her
husband in other areas when he has not been consistent in
leading her spiritually. Therefore, he must learn how to defend
biblical truth against worldly standards in every part of life.
No subject is off limits. Based on continuous work in this area,
at some point, he should fulfill some leadership role within
the local church congregation. Whether it is a high- or low-
profile, role he should be able to serve in some capacity. A man's
commitment to his faith is a determining factor in whether his
children will remain in church after they become adults. He
must be a true example of who Jesus is and teach His Word in
wisdom with instructions for others to follow.

Conclusion

Passing down a righteous legacy begins with choosing the right
wife. Legacy is defined by the choices a man makes and the

women he chooses to mate with. When men do not obey God and are not spiritually strong, whether they are weak, lazy, or cowardly, God responds in judgment by allowing an unnatural and unintended role reversal to take place. This is shown in Scripture where we have a passive, weak man like Ahab and the rising, independent spirit in a woman named Jezebel. A pushover king will always be ruled by a takeover queen. When a man chooses a woman with a Jezebel spirit as his wife, his legacy is finished.

Perpetuating the family name is thought to be an important duty in the hearts of men since eternity is engraved in their hearts (Ecclesiastes 3:11). A legacy is written on our hearts to establish a good reputation that impacts the lives of our children and generations to follow. The legacy we leave in this life is one we lead through the power of the Holy Spirit. This will have an impact on the way we use our words, the way we discipline our children, and the way we love our wives.

God instituted hierarchy in the family for our good. His Word and His example are to be the standard in a Christian home. Not only are husbands to love their wives as Christ loved, but they are to sacrificially give even their lives as He did for all of us. When each member of the family seeks to honor their role as a way of honoring God, the family flourishes, and everyone's needs are met. The transformation in the family will occur once God's design of servant leadership is embraced and followed.

The responsibility of the family rests on the shoulders of the husbands. Remember, the weight of responsibility to lead a family is carried on broad shoulders and not on curvy hips. Men must be able to gauge the physical, emotional, mental, and spiritual temperature of their family. These universal truths are applied to all men in all cultures. God will bless men in their search for suitable wives and a legacy for their children to follow if they diligently seek Him (Hebrews 11:6). Men of God must have the heart to provide and protect. They also must represent their family before God as the priest in the home and represent as God's servant leader to their family as a prophet.

Ruth Ready

Ballroom dancing and all its different variations is a dance activity performed by two people that can be both competitive and social in nature. Leading and following are the key components in social dancing; they are how a dance couple moves together as a unit on the dance floor. The man proposes to dance while it is the woman's choice to accept by following. Ballroom dancing has clear roles: the men are to lead, and the women are to follow as two bodies moving together as one.

The man needs to lead by maintaining the rhythm and deciding what steps are going to be followed. Sometimes he will use his arms to push and pull his partner instead of using his torso to bring an intimate connection with his partner that makes the dancing more synchronized. If the rhythm is off, then there is a great temptation for a woman to resist her role as a follower. She will look over her shoulder to see where she is going or pull her partner in a direction when she does not think he is leading well. This will be an awkward display of dancing when the couples have not learned to work together. They will either step on each other's toes or fight to take the lead. Despite differences in their positions, there are specific steps on the dance floor that must be completed for the routine to work properly.

Boaz took the lead and asked about Ruth (Ruth 2:5). He told Ruth not to glean anywhere else; she would get all she needed from him (Ruth 2:8-9). He even instructed his men who were working in the fields not to touch her (Ruth 2:15). Boaz maintained his godly integrity because he wanted to do what was in Ruth's best interest by provision and protection while expecting nothing in return.

Ruth was leading a life headed for destruction until she decided to follow Jesus. Things did not change for the better for Ruth until she left everything with Naomi for the redemption of Boaz. This is called faith. Ruth clinging to Naomi was her preview to being a wife even when times look bleak. The transformation in Ruth's life did not occur until she was committed to God according to these verses:

> 16But Ruth said: "Entreat me not to leave you,
> Or to turn back from following after you;
> For wherever you go, I will go;
> And wherever you lodge, I will lodge;
> Your people shall be my people,
> And your God, my God.
> 17Where you die, I will die,
> And there will I be buried.
> The LORD do so to me, and more also,
> If anything but death parts you and me."
> (Ruth 1:16-17 NKJV)

Ruth was influenced by Naomi in following God and leaving everything from her native homeland. She wanted to be the daughter of the King instead of searching for a king. Naomi's wise counsel told Ruth to lie at Boaz's feet as a sign of her desire to seek his protection (Ruth 3:4). Now she was asking Boaz to provide that same protection to her by becoming her husband (see Ezekiel 16:8). Like the father gives away his daughter to the groom, our Heavenly Father gives away Ruth to Boaz, and they

are eventually married to keep the covenant from long ago—
they will eventually become great grandparents of King David
and keeping the Messianic line directly to the birth of Jesus.

Identity Crisis

One of the deepest wounds many women carry from
adolescence to adulthood is either an absent father or a weak
presence of a father figure in their lives. Fathers are supposed
to be the first example of the masculine gender. Their biggest
job is to build their daughters' trust in men and prepare them
as suitable wives for husbands. Fathers have the strongest
influence in the protection of a woman's worth, body image, and
acceptance. Without fathers, women are forever seeking to fill
that void in all the wrong places.

Many of today's modern women complain that gender roles
within the confines of marriage are oppressive, limiting, and
archaic. The media portrays successful women as having a job,
nice vehicles, large homes, and leading a family. Their husbands
are soft, passive, effeminate males whom God does not consider
as mighty men of valor for His Kingdom (Judges 6:12). Not
only that, but women are becoming more dominant and
masculine. There might be males here and there to play with but
no men of God to marry.

Modern women call themselves strong and independent and
say that men are either intimidated or cannot handle their
achievements of degrees, status, and money. These women
believe these achievements make them marriage material. Many
of these women believe they should be the first pick, but they
are not, and they fail to understand why. Men, in general, will
not choose them as wives because these women come with
masculine traits that make them intolerable to men. Men are
disgusted by the masculine traits and energy that many modern
women possess.

These women are breaking glass ceilings and climbing to the mountaintop only to discover it is lonely up there with the pool of marriageable men evaporating quickly. Most of their climb was a timewaster because they hiked up the wrong mountain. They thrived and worked so hard academically and financially with no real men of God to marry. What makes matters worse is that children, especially girls, think this is normal and then grow up repeating this destructive cycle.

This thinking activates women's desire for what is written in Scripture immediately after the Fall: forgetting the roles God created women to be. Independent women are fighting to do everything men can do instead of doing everything men *cannot* do well. No one can serve two masters, being independent and God-dependent at the same time (Matthew 6:24). The problem with pursuing the "having it all" or "doing it all" ideology is that this ideology has its roots in the Garden of Eden. Respect may be shown to bosses, managers, or CEOs of companies, but the desire of a wife to rule over her husband is still in play today (Genesis 3:16).

Sometimes a woman may have a professional career and is known by her maiden name. When she marries there is a concern that clients will no longer recognize her with a new last name. Others believe that taking the husband's last name is making her subservient to a man. Keeping the maiden name emphasizes a woman's independence from a man. "Christian" means follower of Christ, carrying the name of the bridegroom. If we are one with Christ, changing your name to his indicates that you affirm the biblical pattern of your husband being the head of your marriage and household (1 Corinthians 11:3; Ephesians 5).

A high percentage of career women are hesitant to settle and are reluctant to have a marriage and family. They disagree with the biblical roles of a wife and do not want to compete for equality at work and home. Most women are raised to be successful and career minded and not be godly wives and mothers. They crave independence and do not want to feel restricted. A pushover king will always be ruled by a takeover queen. Such a woman will never flourish in her femininity until she steps out of her masculine energy. This is partly why most dating relationships or marriages are broken by women.

Call to Biblical Womanhood

Modern women today are considered independent, empowered, and strong. There is an entire generation of Christian women trying to navigate the troubled waters of Biblical womanhood against the tidal wave of feminism. Being virtuous is on the opposite side of the spectrum as being a feminist. A real Godly woman is not independent, empowered, and strong apart from God. The truth is a God-dependent woman has her worth in Christ alone and avoids self-reliance on her worth. Also, a God-dependent woman can do all things through Christ who gives her strength (Philippians 4:13).

Biblical womanhood is listed in these three areas:

1. Significant and magnificent
2. Soft at all costs
3. Supportive and cooperative

> [10]Who can find a virtuous woman?
> For her price is far above rubies.
> (Proverbs 31:10 KJV)

When she maintains being significant and magnificent,
she must put God first and foremost in her life above anyone and anything else. This woman is so exceptional spiritually that she separates herself from what the culture has to offer (2 Corinthians 6:17). Her belief in God's different roles for men and women in marriage is within her mindset (Ephesians

5:22-33). She maintains a reasonable diet and exercises, which improves her overall health because taking care of the body is the same as taking care of God's temple (1 Corinthians 6:19-20). She strives to guard her heart and body for her wedding day. All these things add to her beauty and speak volumes about her discipline and self-control in all areas of her life.

When she maintains being soft at all costs, she puts on full display the glory of God in ways that are unique to a woman. She is not fighting to do everything a man can do but rather to do everything man cannot do. She is wired to nurture and connect with nurturing traits such as compassion, sensitivity, and kindheartedness (1 Peter 3:4). Compassion is to become an empowering strength in others and not point out weaknesses. The ability to feel the emotions of others is incredible. She brings light when someone is having a rough time. The feeling of the emotional needs of others is remarkable. She gives words of encouragement or an unexpected gift at the right time when needed. Status from this world is beneath her for she knows that degrees, awards, or accomplishments hold no marital or eternal value

When she maintains being supportive and cooperative, she is gracious and willing to serve and look beyond self-interest. With the ability to anticipate the needs of others, she is willing to put herself last. She is selfless in generating peace for sake of living in harmony with one another, which is a wonderful task that glorifies God (1 Peter 3:8). Anticipation for the needs of others is knowing when to step in or to give space. When she does these things, others will be open and share the cares of the day.

She inspires others by being steadfast in prayer even when things are not going right. There is thankfulness for any blessings, knowing others are worse off. Being peaceful with her actions is part of her default mode of character. This agreeable spirit is an asset so valuable that it is worth more than anything that can be purchased. Great thoughts and pleasant reactions are triggered by others in her presence. This dedication of humility is an outward display of the glory of God in many ways.

Husband Selection

Men may initiate the relationship or even propose marriage, but it is up to the women to respond—just like no couple is dancing until a woman says yes when asked. What to look for in a husband is more important than looking for a husband. Women should first look for more spiritual characteristics than natural in a potential husband. Yes, physical attraction, similar interests, complementary strengths and weaknesses, and the desire for children are things to consider. If the only time he is on his knees is proposing and not praying, then there is a problem. He is using his playbook instead of the Holy Book, which is the Bible. God said it is not good for a man to be alone. Unfortunately, these men need to be left alone.

Physical traits must be secondary to the spiritual qualities a woman should look for in a man. A man you can trust, respect, and follow in the path of godliness is of far greater value than a man of good looks, influence, or money. Sure, he must have financial maturity in working to take care of a family. In any case, the true value of a man is his integrity, patience, kindness, and willingness to support you, listen to you, and care for you, regardless of what he earns. It is as not important to marry a man with high financial value as to marry a man that highly values what makes him important.

If men do not have the love of Jesus in their hearts, then women will never get the love that they deserve to receive. The Holy Spirit must take residence inside a potential husband. There are qualities within a man that are prominent in who he is and evident for others to witness. Love and accept him for who he is right now and not what he may become in the future. If he is not a new creature in Christ, then looking for potential is meaningless. This sets up disappointment when expectations are not being met. Men will not always perfectly love and lead their wives. Unrealistic expectations can show an absence of grace. Sometimes grace should be extended through forgiveness because knowing what things should be can make us forget what we are at that moment in our lives (Colossians 3:13).

So, what are some examples of how a man feels respected by his wife? These are common expectations that most men want from the women in their lives. First and foremost, he feels respected when she honors his judgment. This means his knowledge, opinions, and decisions are accepted and not rejected based on a rebuttal. Second, he feels respected when she believes that he can accomplish a specific task. This breeds confidence and reassurance that he can figure things out on his own. Lastly, he feels respected when he is not embarrassed inside or outside his presence with belittling or lashing out. Regardless of the reasons, any issue that needs to be resolved must be done in private behind closed doors and not for the public to see. When a husband feels respected, it is easier for him to sacrificially love what a wife needs. The right man is the one who sacrifices enough to put in work that will show off a woman's value within herself.

Roles of a Biblical Wife

Many modern women believe submission is a negative thing that makes them inferior to men. They believe the roles of a godly woman in marriage are often perceived as being archaic and outdated. The first sin came from a woman (Eve), and redemption came from a woman (Mary) leading to the birth of Christ. The roles of wives are from God and not from man. Every woman who desires to be married is responsible for the position of the wife from these verses:

> 22Wives, submit to your own husbands, as to the Lord. 23For the husband is head of the wife, as also

Christ is head of the church; and He is the Savior of
the body. [24]Therefore, just as the church is subject to
Christ, so let the wives be to their own husbands in
everything. (Ephesians 5:22-24 NKJV)

God's will for the wife is to sacrificially respect, support, and
serve her family. This is nothing saying that husbands will not
need love and wives will not need respect. Husbands will grow
into the marriage better with respect and wives will grow into
the marriage better with love. Love and respect are a package
deal since one does not exist without the other. Unfortunately,
sin has corrupted both the loving headship of the husband and
the willing submission of the wife. And so, the perfect love
founded in the Garden of Eden is replaced by the battle of the
sexes. When it comes to the preparation for marriage, if there
is no respect for husbands and love for wives, then the marriage
will certainly die.

When one is under authority, it does not mean inferiority.
Children are to submit to parents, but parents ought to be
submissive about the needs of their children. Employees are to
submit to employers, but employers should be submissive to
their responsibilities toward their employees. Therefore, wives
are to submit to husbands, but husbands should be submissive to
the needs of their wives. Jesus was totally under the submission
of God the Father, yet he is equal to God. The love of God does
not force our submission, or it would not be true submission. For
women to truly fulfill their calling as biblical wives, they must
embrace their responsibilities to their families as helpmeets,
being honorable, hardworking, and hospitable.

Helpmeet

A wife who is a helpmeet is different from her husband but a
perfect fit for him. She completes him in every way and brings
harmony for the Glory of God. The most ideal situation is for

the potential bride to have her father as the protector or use him as a covering for her heart and body. That means she fully trusts the transfer of security and stability from her father to her husband. She is willing to be covered by carrying his last name before carrying his child. The legacy of a godly family from building a family tree comes from a woman who is truly a helpmeet. Her added value to her husband's life is truly priceless according to this verse:

> [18]And the LORD God said, "It is not good that man should be alone; I will make him a helper comparable to him." (Genesis 2:18 NKJV)

Part of a wife's role as a helpmeet is her willingness to submit to her husband. There are times when we must submit to someone according to a specific type of relationship. Whether it is a judge in court, boss on the job, or police officer during a traffic stop, all of us submit to someone. A helpmeet is a wife dependent on God through her husband. This is not a picture of a wife standing behind or in front of her husband but rather coming alongside him and helping him lead the family in the direction God has for them. A submission is a voluntary yielding to another person in a divinely ordered relationship. It is not forced, but rather it is a choice out of love and obedience to Christ.

Honorable

An honorable wife must be gracious in her conduct through her speech and appearance. She worships God daily in this role through her conduct with her words and her appearance, which sets her apart for all to admire. When it comes to her words, they are like a barometer that measures the level of her husband's confidence. She fights the need to be right with opinions on everything and does not disagree in public, get visibly irritated, or question everything in every circumstance (Proverbs 20:9). None of these things are done in public or posted on social media. A woman who conducts herself with such kindness and class finds that men often respond to her favorably. Meekness is not weakness, but power under control in her speech and appearance according to these verses:

> ³Do not let your adornment be merely outward arranging the hair, wearing gold, or putting on fine apparel ⁴rather let it be the hidden person of the heart, with the incorruptible beauty of a gentle and quiet spirit, which is very precious in the sight of God.
> (1 Peter 3:3-4)

Let us not forget clothes did not exist before sin entered our world. There was no shame and no reason to cover our nakedness. God had to sacrifice an animal in the garden for the atonement of Adam and Eve's sinful condition (Genesis 3:21). There may be a covering of the upper thighs, a rising backside, or a plunging neckline for cleavages to prevent exposure. Not only does a wife dress modestly, but she must possess the spirit of modesty. This means her true character reveals not what is seen outside but rather what is on the inside. The inside of the heart uncovers the true motives that are on the outside. For she knows things that you wear, the people you hang around, and the conversations that you have influence the mind (Romans 12:1-2). She models discretion and virtue, which makes her a suitable companion.

Hard Worker

A wife who is a hard worker goes to work on jobs as if the work is never done. She sets her mind to work and completes it no matter how long it takes, and she makes sure it is done well. Boaz notices how hard-working Ruth is from afar . He observes her diligence in her work and her reputation in the community (Ruth 2:6-7). The role of a hard worker does not prohibit women from working outside the home. However, the Bible does teach that their priorities ought to be in the home.

> ¹⁴Do all things without complaining and disputing,
> ¹⁵that you may become blameless and harmless,
> children of God without fault in the midst of a
> crooked and perverse generation, among whom
> you shine as lights in the world.
> (Philippians 2:14-15 NKJV)

The world hates biblical womanhood and a woman's role in marriage and the family. They believe God's design for men and women in the home is oppressive and outdated. Despite the objectives of some, a virtuous woman who is a hard worker has a heart of a servant in completing work because she fears the Lord (Proverbs 31:30). The physical strength for her required tasks is a beautiful picture of her biblical femininity. She is skilled with multitasking and can schedule a balanced life between home and work that gets things done in a timely matter.

Hospitable

A hospitable wife serves her family and community as part of her responsibility to manage the home. She should be like the keeper of the home. This is not house arrest where she is a prisoner wearing an ankle monitor. Her obedience to the word in this role is managing a household and caring for those in it (Proverbs 31:15). The home offers the most encouragement and support to her family and is the best place for extending hospitality to Christian friends, unbelieving neighbors, and even strangers in some cases (Hebrews 13:2). The stability of the home will be based on the wisdom of the wife according to this verse:

> The wise woman builds her house,
> But the foolish pulls it down with her hands.
> (Proverbs 14:1 NJJV)

The prosperity of the home is in her hands. This creates an opportunity for setting the tone by providing structure, routine, peace, and a place of comfort She is like a thermometer regulating the temperature of the home. She is also the light that guides the home and the love that nurtures it. Prayers come from her in providing stability to the environment when there are Satanic attacks. This is prevention of noisy, chaotic, and stressful conditions that would otherwise disrupt and divide the family life. She sets the environment as open and welcoming, which maintains honor and glory whether it comes from her labor inside or outside of the home.

Conclusion

Men will search high and low for virtuous wives because they are even rarer today (Proverbs 31:10). Standards for women to be Ruth ready are that she is a helpmeet, honorable, hardworking, and hospitable. Such women will attempt to live by the Bible in every part of their lives with or without husbands. These women are true legacy makers. They shape the next generation of men and women with their impact on the hearts and minds of children. Virtuous women put forth great influence in training boys into loving husbands and girls into respectful wives.

Ruth ready is not a popular standard of living for most, but the reward is so much greater. Ruth's greatness did not come through self-centered independence, not through favor and beauty; it came through her commitment to God's purpose for her. She decided to be a dependent daughter of Christ instead of a wife to a husband. God blessed Ruth to be part of the Messianic line by trusting in God alone (Ruth 1:16).

Husbands need to know their wives trust their decision-making and their ability to lead their family. Wives should pray for husbands to lead lovingly and wisely. Wives must be patient so as not to take over authority when things are not getting done. Wives must also love God's divine order of husbands' family leadership more than the pursuit to lead and usurp their husbands' authority. When there is trust, peace, and harmony, it is a win-win situation. Wife support is the life support of any family. Wives can influence husbands by trusting and obeying God's word and teaching this to the next generation.

Before Saying I Do

How many times have we heard the story about a boy meeting a girl as a stranger through certain circumstances? Then they go on a series of "dates" to get to know each other. Next, they slowly become intimate emotionally and physically until one will ask the other to go back to "his or her place" late in the evening. Then they will sit on the couch kissing, touching, and working toward sexual intercourse. After that, one will ask the other to move in to live together. Finally, the status of the new relationship will be shared by family and friends while being updated on social media.

Dinner and a movie today were like dowry payments back in Biblical times. People in the Bible were part of prearranged marriages or betrothal periods. The engagement was an announcement with a dowry payment from the wife-to-be's family to the husband-to-be's family. The betrothal lasted for a year during which time they would not live together, and their faithfulness would be tested. Betrothal was considered as legally binding as marriage, and the couple was considered husband and wife (Matthew 1:19). The betrothal or engagement could only be ended by marriage or divorce.

Today, culture has provided the freedom to emphasize physical attributes, appearance, personal finance, and sexual attraction when looking for someone to marry. Some people do not bother looking for a spouse because their primary goal is establishing a career, having fun, or living their best life. That "best life" consists of having multiple partners, kissing numerous people, and engaging in sexual activity before settling down. Most couples become experts in breaking off relationships more than maintaining them. Modern dating is more casual with a series of trial runs of potential partners that leads to connecting emotionally, physically, or both. These relationships can be considered pseudo-marriages because people give themselves away repeatedly to unworthy candidates who break their hearts. Marriage is just an idea, but it may or may not become a reality. There is no serious thought about marriage.

Time spent as a carefree single is considered a "rite of passage" in our society. It seems this important life stage has been filtered down to the teen and even preteen groups. The words *dating* and *courtship* are not in the Bible, but there are verses about sexual purity and self-control. The following verses are a challenge for anyone who is currently dating:

> 12Therefore do not let sin reign in your mortal body, that you should obey it in its lusts. 13And do not present your members as instruments of unrighteousness to sin but present yourselves to God as being alive from the dead, and your members as instruments of righteousness to God.
> (Romans 6:12-13 NKJV)

A key component of dating is physical intimacy. So, the question remains how much physical interaction? Song of Solomon also warns to "not awaken love before its time" (Song of Solomon 2:7). Sex before marriage is not biblical, therefore each couple will have to make that decision as to how far they can go if they are heading toward the sexual intercourse stage. The word *dating* seems to be the popular term, and *courting* is the least popular term. The term *courtship* is hardly ever used in everyday language. In comparison to dating, courtship tends to be less self-centered and more others-centered where marriage is the goal. Since the word *courting* is hardly ever used, we will use the terms *Christian dating* and *modern dating* for the duration of this chapter.

Online vs. Real-Life Dating

People use all types of methods of finding a spouse. In today's digital age, almost half of new relationships start online. Online dating is just one of the methods to choose when considering modern dating. This includes emails, texting, social media, and numerous dating apps. People are clicking, swiping, or scrolling on electronic devices looking for that special someone for a loving relationship. Everyone wants to love and to be loved. Relationships have become more like technology: We want instant results without any effort to sustain our attention.

As of 2020, online dating is the most popular method of dating to meet people. Getting together is one thing, but marriage is something else. Yet, there are specialists in this area who boast success stories of marriage that came from meeting singles online. I do understand we must change with the times or get left behind; however, the abundance of candidates online does not necessarily make it better. Just like internet information, the vetting process poses a serious challenge in weeding out who is the right or wrong type of person to consider dating. Virtual profiles and video screens must eventually give way to a real-life, face-to-face-meeting.

Using technology to find potential marriage partners has its pros and cons. On one hand, we have easy access to information. This includes a numerous list of potential partners to choose from. Their habits, lifestyle, and age are analyzed for possible matches.

So, in one respect, online dating is merely a tool God can use to bring two people together. On the other hand, there is an issue with the lack of detailed information. Deception is common with online dating sites, and people hide behind their profiles to prevent being hurt or rejected. It is tricky to tell who is honest and who is pretending to be someone else. The fact of the matter is that looking for love online betrays a lack of faith in God's provision of a spouse. Choose wisely when deciding whether to use this option when finding potential mates.

When it comes to real-life dating, the person is a real human with a name and body compared to photos and a few messages on some profile. Before online dating, people had to venture out to public places like college campuses, nightclubs, or work, or get set up through friends and family. Every encounter of meeting someone for dating purposes should have the intention of marriage, but not every relationship will necessarily lead to marriage. Any breakup or rejection should not leave one fearful of trying again. Also, we cannot be lazy by sitting back and waiting on God to "reveal" that one destined to be our spouse. We can put ourselves in a position to meet single people.

Consider Ruth: she boldly put herself in a position to meet Boaz. She did not initiate the meeting with conversation or chase after him. As stated earlier, online dating is one method, and some people prefer to meet their potential spouses through friends, family, church services, conferences, or in a chance meeting out in the world. Some believe they are limited in the people they meet because of their profession, where they live, or their activities outside of work. In life, there are things we cannot control for time, and circumstances happen to us all (Ecclesiastes 9:11).

Which is the best method of meeting singles for potential marriage? When it comes to finding spouses, the Bible does not directly tell us how to find our spouses. According to different passages of the Bible, Abraham had his chief servant find a wife for his son, Isaac. King Xerxes held a beauty contest before landing Esther as his queen. King David had a man killed before taking that man's wife, Bathsheba, as his own. Even Moses was given Zipporah after he impressed her father while watering his flock and protecting the women from radical shepherds. The truth is that there are no clear-cut directions in the Bible for finding spouses. Whatever method is selected to find potential spouses, we must conclude there is no shortage of people to date, but there is a severe shortage of datable people.

The biggest challenge for me before I was married was that I tried to do everything on my own. I understood that God has given us absolute, independent, free moral agency to execute our choices, and I wanted to take full advantage of this without help. God is sovereign, and His will controls all events directly or indirectly for His purposes. His direct will overrides man's will when it goes against His plan. God's indirect will allows mankind to follow their wills and desires, which usually end up in a bad outcome. It is always best to do things His way and leave the results to Him. All things are done for our good and His glory (Romans 8:28).

Red Flags

In relationships heading for marriage, it is vitally important to recognize what are called red flags. Red flags are warning signs that could come into question in the future based on past behaviors. Everyone has red flags to some extent because of imperfections in our character as humans. Someone's past is not automatically a red flag, especially if they have taken steps to change through repentance. None of us are any good because all of us need salvation through Jesus Christ (Romans 3:12). Potential mates will not check all the boxes to meet all the standards we look for in a future spouse. Every spouse will marry a sinner with a past, and our spouse will marry a sinner as well.

There are dealbreakers to look for before entering a permanent relationship. Dealbreakers are more significant than red flags because they cannot be ignored. They are certain nonnegotiable factors that will cause the relationship to end immediately. It is important for couples to into marriage with both eyes open. Keep in mind that dealbreakers may not be visible until after the wedding takes place. When it comes to choosing a spouse, we must seek God's counsel. Other than daily prayers and the study of His word, a third-party Christian counseling professional should be considered before and after the wedding. They should be considered especially when there are any potential marriage issues. Christian counselors are placed on Earth to help those in need.

Even though the Bible does not use the terms *red flags* or *dealbreakers*, it does tell us how to relate to one another, especially in serious relationships that are heading for marriage. The most important trait to look for in a spouse is a genuine love for God. This is showing reverence for how we faithfully live by putting God first in everything and obeying His commands through His Word. Because there is no specific list of red flags, it is important to mention two dealbreakers. First and foremost, not sharing the same faith should immediately terminate the relationship. Our souls are on the line, and with this following verse, spiritual compatibility must always be at the top of our list:

> 14Do not be unequally yoked together with unbelievers.
> For what fellowship has righteousness with lawlessness?
> And what communion has light with darkness?
> (2 Corinthians 6:14 NKJV)

No unbeliever will be able to do God's will in marriage unless the heart is changed by Him. This verse is a command and not a request. It further discusses how the nonbeliever can influence the believer's thinking. When a believer chooses to date or marry a nonbeliever, that person has put themselves in danger by compromising their faith. Compromising for the good of the relationship is acceptable if both people will benefit. However, compromising standards that do not align with Scripture for the sake of love, peace, or getting one's way is never the answer. Relationships work better in harmony when couples walk in agreement and togetherness while practicing the same faith (Amos 3:3).

The second dealbreaker is just as important as the first. We should be mindful of controlling manipulative behaviors. This can lead to some sort of physical and emotionally abusive behaviors. Some of the preferences on a given list have nothing to do with whether this is a great candidate for a husband or wife. Using a variety of lists from online sources, in books, or from dating gurus can be overwhelming. It is always better for the Bible to speak for itself because it is the only book that judges us. The following verses list what kind of people to avoid altogether, especially when considering them for marriage:

> ²For men will be lovers of themselves, lovers of money, boasters, proud, blasphemers, disobedient to parents, unthankful, unholy, ³unloving, unforgiving, slanderers, without self-control, brutal, despisers of good, ⁴traitors, headstrong, haughty, lovers of pleasure rather than lovers of God, ⁵having a form of godliness but denying its power. And from such people turn away!
> (2 Timothy 3:2-5 NKJV)

All of us have demonstrated some of these behaviors, but none of us should be living a lifestyle of these behaviors. These verses serve as an excellent starting point to weed out the pretenders from the contenders for marriage. These warning signs help prevent a dating or engaged relationship from becoming a heartbreaking marriage that would most likely be ending in divorce. All of us carry some baggage. They are habits, frailties, and flaws within a person that makes them who they are when the spotlight is not shining on them. Are we able to accept the baggage that comes with the person we plan on marrying?

Although the actions of others cannot be controlled because of their behaviors, it is imperative to choose right the first time. There must be an understanding that only two outcomes exist for dating relationships: getting married or breaking up. Before the walk down the marriage aisle, there are many things we can consider. In this chapter, we will cover seven matters to consider before marriage. These suggestions help recognize if the relationship should move forward toward marriage.

Character

There are two types of people: kingdom minded (Christ) and carnal minded (culture). The person in question must be a follower of Christ. The character of a prospective spouse will make married life heaven or hell; it gives a glimpse before marriage leading up to the time after marriage. Many want to know about getting to know someone and eventually getting married without being hurt in the process. Marriage only changes a person's status, not their character.

Getting to know someone should be based on character and not personality. Personality is who we are when the spotlight is on. We show different sides we want people to believe. We tend to show only the best of ourselves and hide what is not desirable. This is how we are on our best behavior at the beginning of the relationship but then change based on the situation and circumstances. Even choosing a partner for personality traits does not compare with character traits.

Character is who we are inside of us because of our relationship with Christ. It is something that can be built and learned as we follow Him. It brings about the fruit of the spirit. It is impossible to plan for a successful godly marriage without planting the fruits of the spirit. These characteristics based on the fruits of the Spirit are found in the following verses:

22But the fruit of the Spirit is love, joy, peace, longsuffering, kindness, goodness, faithfulness, 23gentleness, and self-control. Against such, there is no law. (Galatians 5:22-23 NKJV)

We often want to reap a harvest before planting seeds in our relationships. Our relationship with Christ will bring about the fruit of the Spirit. The evidence of His presence in our lives will be observed by others. Character is also influenced by our choices. The friends in our circle are a strong indicator. We can be persuaded by those we spend time together with (1 Corinthians 15:33). The way we respond in stressful situations reflects who we are. It also determines how we communicate.

Communication

God designed men and women to be different. When it comes to communication, there must be a clear understanding of the differences between the way men and women communicate. Recognizing these differences can strengthen the relationship as couples enter marriage. Men tend to focus on facts, think about one issue at a time, and have a strong desire to make decisions in solving problems. Women tend to emphasize the feelings behind the facts, talk through problems with someone, and want to talk about how they feel. Consequently, men listen to women when they are sharing their thoughts and feelings, and women give their men time to process information to come up with solutions. In Christian dating relationships, it is necessary to improve the skill of godly communication as prescribed in the following verses:

31Let all bitterness, wrath, anger, clamor, and evil speaking be put away from you, with all malice. 32And be kind to one another, tenderhearted, forgiving one another, even as God in Christ forgave you. (Ephesians 4:31-32 NKJV)

Like death, there is absolute certainty someone will irritate you within a given relationship. This is part of human nature, especially when it is necessary to determine whether this is the right person for marriage. It is important to have enough common interests to enjoy spending time together. Communication fosters trust and transparency with no hidden agendas. There should be a desire to examine character based on previous relationships and history. A failure to be open about weaknesses and struggles with your partner before marriage will become more difficult afterward. Sometimes truth is withheld from past sinful behaviors or painful experiences. A couple preparing for marriage has a right to know much of what occurred to the other person. This includes but is not limited to prior sexual experiences, transmitted diseases, abortions, and any type of abuse that should be known before a marriage takes place. An opportunity should be made for a potential partner to get a sneak peek of how life has shaped the character of the person in a future marriage. Before we initiate the process of marriage, dig deeper to see just how deep these issues are and whether any baggage can be endured for a lifetime.

We all have bad days and sometimes make mistakes. Sometimes an uncertain environment is created that makes it difficult to solve problems or openly talk with each other. There are usually two types of responses that couples cannot handle at the start of conflict: outbursts of temper or long periods of silence. Pride is the source of conflicts that cause arguments because of perceived unmet needs. In every relationship, pride is the fruit, and sin is the root. The ability to handle conflicts at the start of disagreement and ending with a resolution will be critical to the success or failure of the marriage.

Prayer is the most powerful thing you can do to prepare for marriage. It will be a key factor that gets you both through the hardest times. God must be invited in every situation, in good or bad seasons. Many times, it is more important to *listen* than to talk and to fight the urge to be right (James 1:19). There is a temptation for us to fix things ourselves without His help, which usually leads to bad results. Being able communicate hard truths as to what they are witnessing with a prospective spouse is a union that can lead to a lifelong commitment.

Community

Community is like a warm circle surrounded by a godly council of family members, mentors, and close friends. It makes no sense to find a mate alone with no guidance or supervision. There are emotional blinders (seeing for who the person really is) that can prevent seeing if the person they are dating is marriage material. No one should marry without any input from the family. Couples are personally involved in the relationship with an already established bias. Beyond daily prayer and study of the Word, wise counsel should be considered for a question regarding the stability of an impending marriage. This verse Solomon wrote reminds us of the wisdom of involving others:

[22]Without counsel, plans go awry,
But in the multitude of counselors, they are established.
(Proverbs 15:22 NKJV)

Surround yourself with people who consider the LORD worthy of our obedience and know His word. Seek an older, more experienced married couple to provide wisdom and support to prepare you for your adventure together leading to marriage. Note that couples will have that feeling of "being in love," but at times it hides each's true character. Therefore, each mate should be interviewed and tested as proof to verify an ideal marriage candidate.

The goal here is to confirm the relationship through parents and others. In the process, the family will make careful observations and opinions of a prospect as they watch the person more closely. They are supposed to tell the truth in love about the condition of the relationship. It is vitally important to pay close attention to the family's findings and listen to the lessons learned during their years of marriage and manage expectations. Be wise to spend much more time in marriage preparation than in wedding planning. Blessings are easier to obtain when the family has an opportunity to spend time with the potential spouse. So, both partners need to have a spiritual growth mindset and a commitment to each other.

Commitment

Christian singles who are marriage minded must be committed to each other and build an intimate connection. Without connection, there is no commitment. Knowing the person beyond the surface level is key. Commitment is a promise that requires a connection for the right reasons. The connection is a closeness not just for physical reasons but emotional and spiritual reasons as well.

There must be a prior discussion on the relationship being defined as monogamous with intentions of refraining from sexual activity until marriage (Hebrews 13:4). Commitment is a choice to believe in the assurance of a future marriage. This type of Christian relationship must have follow-through and commitment to stay together over the long haul. It requires work and a lot of time. This is how men become husbands before marriage and women become wives before marriage. The following verse tells us the outcome of the relationship depends on how much work is put in:

> ⁹And let us not be weary in well doing:
> for in the due season, we shall reap if we faint not.
> (Galatians 6: KJV)

Marriage will be more about commitment than compatibility. It is a daily choice to say yes, even in the face of hardship and adversity. After all, there has never been a less compatible relationship than a holy God and His sinful bride, the Israelites. Therefore, God used Hosea as a metaphor for His relationship with Israel when he told him to marry a prostitute (Hosea 1:2). The type of commitment God has for His people is what we should be aiming for in our marriages. Commitment is acceptance of God's expectations of how men and women complete each other in relationships.

Composition

Composition is the makeup or the structure of a relationship by accepting who they are without trying to change each other. However, modern Western society is moving toward treating men and women as social equals with no distinction of roles within marriage. Sadly, the word *egalitarian* is often used by many people in relationships. Part of the problem is the misinterpretation of Ephesians 5:21, which says," Submit to one another out of reverence for Christ." The misreading merges submission in the church between members along with submission in Christian marriages between husbands and wives. Christ does not submit to His bride, and marriage is a metaphorical illustration of Christ and the Church. This is bending the Bible to fit the world's standards.

Each mate has been shaped by his or her personal history, and both have wounds from the past. Respecting each person's differences is showing love (1 Peter 4:8). The blending of two people coming together as one is a very difficult concept to achieve. The foundation for marriage is laid during the Christian dating period, not after the wedding day. With the right fit, there must be an improvement within the relationship because of godly influence. Men and women are incomplete without the other because they are created to complement one another (Genesis 2:18).

Composition is also accepting unique roles that God has set for both men and women in a marriage. God created men and women equal in their being, dignity, and worth (Galatians 3:28) but different in role and function. When it comes to God-given roles—especially as it pertains to the family—the Bible is clear about the different functions associated with each gender. These roles are God's design from the beginning of creation and *before* the fall of mankind. Paul wrote this specifically for church leadership, but it is also in a marriage relationship in this verse:

> ³But I want you to know that the head of every man is Christ, the head of the woman is man, and the head of Christ is God.
> (1 Corinthians 11:3 NKJV)

Men are not superior, and women are not inferior, but God has set this divine order in a marriage relationship. Even Christ submits to the Father. This is what makes each couple suitable instead of compatible. The Bible used the word *suitability* (Genesis 2:18). There must be the right fit with the purpose for God's glory in the union. We must be careful of worshipping the God of marriage and not the marriage of God. Husbands are given the responsibility by God for servant leadership of the family and wives the responsibility to help them.

Cash Management

Cash Management is handling spending and budgeting along with merging assets and debts. The responsibility here is to take care of the present needs of the family. When exploring the possibility of marriage, remember that love does not pay the bills. Money is one of the biggest things that couples argue about. Marriage is supposed to be more important than money. Financial conflict is the second leading cause of divorce. The root of mismanagement of money is selfishness according to these verses:

³Let nothing be done through selfish ambition or conceit, but in lowliness of mind let each esteem others better than himself. ⁴Let each of you look out not only for his own interests but also for the interests of others.
(Philippians 2:3-4)

Financial decisions that impact the success of the family are a shared responsibility. Each person brings his or her ideas about how money should be spent in the marriage. They also have different ideas about accumulating debt or sticking to a regular budget. With money, it always boils downs to either spending or saving. There is a balance between being careful and concerned about saving for later or living for the moment and spending. There must be protection against reckless spending by not living above means. Respect is shown to the household finances when there is self-control in spending habits. Whatever the source of God's provisions, the assets accumulated are the responsibility of both partners together as a team.

People forget money does not truly belong to us. Money and everything in this world belong to God (Psalm 24:1). Once we die, we cannot take it with us. We return to the ground as dust (Ecclesiastes 3:20). There will be expectations as stewards to manage His property according to His principles and standards. This includes giving, saving, investing, and leaving an inheritance. We must be mindful not to place importance on material things above God. Otherwise, these things will become idols. No income is guaranteed to last forever, and we are promised that money is not the key to happiness. We can't take our things with us into Heaven, but we can use finances to be a blessing to others while still living here (1 Timothy 6:7).

Children

Children must be discussed as to how many are wanted and how to train them by disciplining them. Discipline on the part of a soon-to-be-married couple of when to reproduce is very important. Pregnancy spacing is an essential part of family planning because it entails the number and timing of the children to be born. Children come with a cost; they are an asset to the family but an expense in the family budget. Others reproduce children without any planning, not considering the cost, effort, time, or wisdom needed. Either way, the goal is still to get them all to adulthood with strong Christian character, productive careers, and seeking godly spouses.

Most people base their parenting ideas on the way they were raised. When two people were brought up with very different parenting styles, there could be a communication breakdown when they start their family. There must be an agreement when it comes to training up children. This verse assures us that with proper training, children will live a life that is pleasing to God:

> 6Train up a child in the way he should go,
> And when he is old he will not depart from it.
> (Proverbs 22:6 NKJV)

This verse is a commandment with a promise. Children do not come with directions, but they do come with instructions. The Bible gives instructions on the stages of child development. Instructions in the training of children simply mean shaping or perfecting moral character. Healthy discipline includes guiding them and correcting them. With guidance, the children will know how to conduct themselves and make good decisions. There are times when children will disappoint, so correction is necessary. Foolishness is bound in the heart of children, so corrective discipline is mandatory, and this includes spanking (Proverbs 22:15).

Children need hope beyond this fallen world. They must live a life of faith with eternity in mind. Children must also be taught how to pray and witness praying from the adults in the home. This truth about rearing children must be passed down from one generation to the next. This means families staying together for a lifelong commitment to God while raising children to repeat the cycle for the next generation. Our children are currently in the middle of a spiritual battle in enemy territory. Parents must teach children to follow Christ, or the world will teach them not to.

Conclusion

Christian dating, unlike modern dating, is not meant to be conducted over many years. Although there are no clear-cut answers found in the Bible as to how long the dating period should be before marriage, dating is meant to be a brief time to see if the couple is suitable for marriage. Typically, this process is meant to be a a few months but usually does not go beyond a year. Too many people are pursuing the moment and not the result, which is marriage. So much time has been wasted.

For those who are considering marriage, when one marries another, each one is also marrying the in-laws along with the extended family. Also, when marrying someone, do not forget any possible underlying hereditary issues that are part of the biological makeup. This person may be a carrier of a serious genetic disorder that attacks the mind, heart, blood, or bones. All these possible issues are remnants of the Fall in the Garden of Eden (Genesis 3). Do not expect perfection based on some checklist we have in our minds. We cannot put demands on others that we cannot live with ourselves.

God's ways are always higher than our ways, and they serve a purpose. He sees things tomorrow that we cannot today. That is precisely why we can trust Him and His timing, especially when concerning such an important decision as to whom we plan to share our lives with. Time and patience must set in to learn about the potential marriage partner (James 1:4). When someone seeks perfection in a potential spouse, they will always be disappointed. Perfection is not about finding the perfect one in our lives but the one who fits in our lives perfectly.

Covenant or Contract

Next to the acceptance of God through Jesus Christ as Lord and Savior, whom we marry will be the most important decision we will ever make in our lives. Marriage is the first of the three divine institutions created by God. The other two divine institutions are the church and government. Not only the home was established before the church, but God also established marriage between a man and a woman (Genesis 2:24). God is so serious about marriage that the marriage analogy is often used in the relationship between Himself and the Israelites in the Old Testament and the relationship of Christ and the Church in the New Testament of the Bible. The institution of marriage helps with the church and government, which were all established by God for our good and His glory.

In all cultures, weddings are a time of great joy for all involved. Weddings are also a time of new beginnings and a time when the couple commits their lives together as one. Here in the Western part of the world, planning for a wedding is like a double-edged sword. Many couples buy into the lie of the wedding day because it has become so self-centered. Budgeting for a wedding may include food, flowers, music, venues, and a wedding dress. A wedding day is considered a successful one when everyone serves the newly married couple.

The promotional advertisement focuses on the wedding day and brides exclusively. Too much attention is given to the bride and very little to the groom as the newly married couple. Grooms are perceived as unwilling Neanderthals who are dragged to the altar kicking and screaming. There is too much emphasis on the wedding and not on the marriage. Over half of the marriages will become costly when they end in divorce, and the brides will file approximately 80 percent of them.

There is a great difference when planning for a wedding and marriage. Planning for a wedding only lasts for one day, while marriage will be for many days, hopefully a lifetime. An illusion was created that marriage is the end goal of all relationships. While the attention of the impending marriage will be focused on the couple, Christ is not the central part of the wedding ceremony in most cases.

God is not the author of confusion, we are (1 Corinthians 14:33). We have written stories in our lives where we set limitations on God's expectations before the wedding day. All the wedding planning details do not compare with the character details of the couple and the merging of their families. Confessing in being a Christian does not guarantee a long-lasting marriage either. The root of sin has destroyed marriages in both believers and nonbelievers alike.

What is marriage anyway? There is no full agreement from people outside of the Christian faith on what is the definition of marriage. The definition of marriage is difficult to answer on our own because it has multiple meanings. According to the latest definition from Merriam-Webster (2009), marriage is "the state of being united as spouses in a consensual and contractual relationship recognized by law." However, the book of Genesis explains the definition of marriage clearly in the following verses:

> And the rib, which the LORD God had taken from
> man, made he a woman and brought her unto the
> man And Adam said, this is now bone of my bones,
> and flesh of my flesh: she shall be called Woman
> because she was taken out of Man. Therefore, shall a
> man leave his father and his mother, and shall cleave
> unto his wife: and they shall be one flesh.
> (Genesis 2:22-24 NKJV)

Adam and Eve had a perfect marriage in a perfect world. Unfortunately, they thought they had a better idea and decided to go beyond God's rules as sin entered the picture. Anything that alters God's will for us is an invention by man. There is a great divide in the outlook of marriage between what the Bible says and what man says. When it is time for us to marry, we must understand there are only two types of marriages: those that honor God and those that do not. This leads to comparing two types of marriages: covenant and contract. A contract marriage is when God is nonexistent, and its foundation is based on human philosophies that are integrated with the laws of the land. Covenant marriage is when God is front and center of the union. He is the initiator and creator of marriage with the foundation that comes from the Bible. Most modern marriages are contract marriages.

No matter what type of marriage, couples are expected to commit to one another and continue to grow together as one. It must be understood that the couple decides to leave their parents and cleave to one another as a new family takes a higher priority than the old family (Genesis 2:24). Couples must plan to show their devotion to each other through marriage. Marriages will begin with the best intentions of staying together until death. It will be challenging when two people who come from different backgrounds are expected to live together in harmony for life. Before anyone considers marriage, a decision must be made to consider either a contract or covenant marriage.

First, we will examine their similarities and then the differences between the two.

At the outset, both contract and covenant marriages are recognized as public institutions that involve governing and legal matters such as a license with signatures or a seal by the given nation (Genesis 2:23-24). It is a vow of lifetime commitment by two people to spend their lives together as married partners through a ceremony usually with friends and family (Mark 10:6-9). In other words, this is the beginning of a new life and an adventure of two people joining their lives together. This lifetime commitment includes sexual fidelity, meaning sex between the couple within the marriage and not outside the marriage. The vow within a given marriage is the heartbeat of the union. The vows are said by couples and heard by all present.

Marriage will also be a financial matter. Financial decisions that impact the success of the family are a shared responsibility. There is support required where there are comingling of funds and resources to secure family needs like food, clothing, and shelter. Family income and earnings belong to the family and not to the individual. There must be an agreement with spending, saving, assets, and expenses along with roles and responsibilities. Communication and working together in this area are keys to holding the marriage together.

The Bible does not require weddings to take place in a specific location concluding in a church ceremony. Couples must decide if they will incorporate religious institutions such as a church, synagogue, preacher, and Holy verses into the ceremony. Another choice is to have the event outside the traditional use of religious institutions and use a judge or other public official to perform the ceremony in other settings. There are several forms of wedding ceremonies besides the traditional church ceremony. Generally, there is no specific order in the wedding ceremony, but they typically include these basic parts that tend to be the same:

- Wedding processional or entrance of the groom, wedding party, and bride
- Reading of some kind (e.g., vows poetry, or Scriptures)
- Witnesses (family and friends)
- Exchange of rings and/or gifts
- First kiss as a married couple
- A recessional (the exit of new married couple, wedding party, and family)

This general list is usually common in most weddings in both traditional and nontraditional settings. Typically, from the processional to the recessional, most of these elements are parts of a typical wedding ceremony, but there may be variations here and there. Remember, any soon-to-be-married couple can always add and omit some parts as they see fit.

Now that we've looked at similarities, let's consider differences between seeing marriage as a contract as opposed to a covenant. To understand marriage as a contract, we need to recognize what makes a contract different from a covenant. Sometimes these terms are used interchangeably, and the word *covenant* is used less frequently. The key component in determining what kind of marriage we want or are currently in is our mindset. This means our attitude while in the marriage has a direct outcome at the end of a marriage. There are only two results: death or divorce. We can enter marriage to go along with the world or change the world as a living testimony for God's glory. There are fundamental differences between a modern-day contract and a biblical covenant.

Contract

When considering contract marriage, it is more of a financial business decision than an emotional one. It has little to do with "true love," "falling in love," "soul mates," or any inner connection at all. Marriage is intended for a life-long commitment and requires a great deal of forethought before this decision is made. Love is not the reason or even required in a contract marriage. This is more of a financial business decision, an exchange of what each person can provide.

Investment in a business or becoming a partner has risks and rewards. A comprehensive summary of time and income takes place, analyzing the protection of current and future assets. Net worth on the balance sheets that list current assets and liabilities is essential. Parties must fit together by utilizing their expertise in areas where there are weaknesses. In other words, what is in it for me, and how can my time and money increase to their greatest potential? The number of resources available based on income sets the terms of the relationship.

Choosing marriage is like an entrepreneur picking a company to invest in. Marriage is an exchange of resources. Person A will provide this, and Person B will provide that. If either party does not or will not provide his or her share, then the marriage should end. Marriage of this type is like investing resources to secure benefits, hoping to receive a payoff later. It is a contractual agreement between two individuals that satisfactorily benefits both parties that are grounded in negotiation. Like businesses, there must be full disclosure of all assets and liabilities before the marital agreement is made.

A contract marriage is when two people have decided they want to be married and spend their life together, and their marriage is recognized by the government. The state has the authority to define marriage however it wants because marriage is simply a legal arrangement administered by law. No religious institution is necessary to officiate the wedding ceremony. The attitude here is that the union is held by a piece of paper signed by an official from a given state.

A marriage contractual mindset can be problematic when it comes to longevity. There was a time when there was respect for the importance and permanence of marriage. Unfortunately, today when people enter marriage there is a mindset of assuming that if it doesn't work out, they can always end it. When people marry it is by choice. Free choice, in many cases here, means being freed from Biblical principles. People can marry or leave anyone at any time for any reason.

Within contract marriages, agreements are contingent on both parties holding up their ends. A contract marriage becomes active "until you do something to me that I don't like." Failure to perform duties within the contract is highlighted due to performance from one or both parties. This contract can be torn up at will. It is disposable when agreements become disagreements. When this happens, forgiveness is not required, and the relationship can be terminated. These differences lead to things like no-fault divorce.

There are so many stories of wealthy people such as celebrities or athletes getting married and then divorcing in less than five years. A marriage contract covers the perception of what could happen. This leads to an option within contract marriages that creates safeguards necessary to protect assets in case of divorce. A legal option called a prenuptial agreement is where couples make clear written expectations of financial matters of division of assets when the marriage is over. The value of prenups is in its transparency by setting expectations of the marriage from the very beginning. Independence is the priority in contract marriages. Couples will agree to work together until there is a belief that divorce is an option. This gives the initiator of this agreement a choice to exercise an escape route in case things do not work out.

Additional clauses that can be added to the prenup are called lifestyle clauses. They have become increasingly popular among those who are not celebrities or athletes. This is an additional clause within prenups for couples to be creative in expressing needs and working together to set boundaries within their relationship. Every clause is not always a financial matter, but it can be tied to a financial penalty for breaking it. These lifestyle clauses address non-financial aspects of the marriage—for example, who will do the housework, the frequency of sex, the permissible number of visits from in-laws, and even weight requirements. Sometimes this type of marriage agreement can be revisited when life circumstances change.

When conflict arises, conditions may change within the relationship in a contract marriage. Divorce is considered a right by man even though God hates divorce (Malachi 2:15). Aside from adultery, abuse, or addiction, if one agreeing party does something in violation of the contract, then it is considered broken. The whole contract becomes null and void. Legal representatives will have to negotiate to settle the financial terms with alimony, child custody, and property. No moral stigma is attached, and divorcing parties can move on with their lives.

Happiness is the fruit and self-centeredness is the root behind contractual marriages. This type of marriage is treated more like a business partnership as the terms for dissolving the partnership are when the couple is no longer happy with the arrangement. "As long I am satisfied with what I can get, there will be no problems in the marriage." In a contract marriage, commitment is contingent entirely upon feelings. However, if one or both parties decide it is better to break up the marriage to find someone new, they will be able to escape their current situation and try again and find a more compatible partner with whom they believe they can build a better life.

There's no consequence or higher authority to answer to in this type of marriage. Therefore, belief in God is not required (Psalm 14:1). The contract type of marriage does not invite God into the relationship. Either party can walk away from this type of marriage, especially when conditions change as in income loss and sickness. Contract marriage focuses on what the creature wants and not following what the Creator says is best.

Covenant

Today in our culture we have lost the understanding of the meaning of covenants. We only think of marriage in terms of contracts. In our minds, all our agreements are contingent on both parties holding up their ends. However, there are differences between a modern-day contract and a biblical covenant. A covenant is more intimate and personal than a business-type relationship. For us to better understand marriage as a covenant, we need to understand what makes a covenant different from a contract.

When referring to a covenant marriage in this book, I am referring to the spirit of the term and not the letter of it. In other words, the Bible is the final authority that goes beyond any laws passed by a government. We must keep in mind that God will judge according to the spirit of the law, not just the letter. Covenant marriage is God's plan and can never be lasting without His perfect will. There may be segments of contractual marriage woven in and out within the confines of covenant marriage, but for the Christian, marriage is a covenant. Two people make a vow to serve one another and make this promise before God. A covenant is like a contract, though a covenant is bound specifically by an oath before God. We must invite God to be the center of our marriages. Marriage is not forever. Simply put, it is a commitment that ends at death.

God's covenant of love with Israel and His covenant of love with His church, the Bride of Christ, are reflections of old and new testaments of what marriage is supposed to be. Christ is represented as the bridegroom, and the church is represented as His Bride. The church submits to Christ because He suffered and died for her (Ephesians 5:25). This is required from husbands in the same way for their wives. Contract marriages, where there is a partnership between couples, do not exist in a true covenant marriage. The latter is what God has established.

Marriage to an unbeliever is never a good idea because this is not how God designed marriage in the first place (1 Corinthians 7:39). Believers should marry believers, and both spouses must live as best as possible as outlined in Scripture (2 Corinthians 6:14). Samson and Solomon's marriages serve us as a reminder of how easily we can be led away from God by marrying unbelievers. The marriage union is a dress rehearsal of the union between Christ and the Church (Revelation 19:7-9). This is the ultimate marriage. There is no giving into marriage after the end times. We are united with Christ in the bonds of love forever if we choose to accept Him as Lord and Savior.

Adam and Eve formed the first covenant with one another before God (Genesis 2:22-24). Since then, believers have emulated this idea of marriage. A covenant is like a contract, though a covenant is bound specifically by an oath before God. This covenant is a trifold *relationship* between a man, a woman, and God. The union must become one in everything—physically, spiritually, and relationally. How important is marriage to Jesus anyway? It was held in high regard when He turned water into wine at a wedding party (John 2: 7-9).

> Have you not read that He who made them at the beginning 'made them male and female,' and said, 'For this reason, a man shall leave his father and mother and be joined to his wife, and the two shall become one flesh? So then, they are no longer two but one flesh. Therefore, what God has joined together, let not man separate.
> (Matthew 19:4-6)

This verse makes marriages both natural and spiritual. Jesus had to remind everyone of the first marriage between Adam and Eve by quoting Genesis 2:24. This establishes the first divine institution. Then Jesus stated the shifted loyalty from parents to the spouse. This means parents are moved from the front of the line to the back of the line and the couple must lean on each other, not their parents. God's marriage and perfect plan for us are for a husband and wife to be committed to each other until the death of either party. God expects our marriage covenant to last forever with the death of one or both persons.

A covenant marriage is based on mutual trust set by principles from the Word of God. Life has ever-changing conditions, but the responsibility within marriage is unchangeable during up and down seasons. The couples are interdependent with each other and dependent on God until He takes one of them out of the world through death. So, divorce should never be an option. Conflicts will occur in marriage, and differences must be worked out through prayer, forgiveness, and sacrifice. This is the real love that grows over time.

Happiness and companionship in a covenant marriage are not the end goal. They are desirable benefits of marriage but not the purpose of marriage. The world wants to redesign marriage on its terms. A strong, godly marriage is offensive to the world that hates God in the first place because it convicts their sinful lifestyles. God gives three purposes for covenant marriage: to reflect, reproduce, and reign. Because of the importance of these purposes, Satan works hard to keep Christians from accomplishing them.

First, God created marriage and family to advance God's kingdom through reflecting the image of God and exercising dominion over the Earth (see Genesis 1:28). This image is the starting point of the divine relationship between Christ and the Church (Ephesians 5:31–33). This is the blueprint for men and women to copy this illustration when they decide to marry. When God designed Eve, it was to complete what was missing in Adam's life since it was not good for him to be alone. Marriage is to be a covenant between a couple for God to symbolize and declare their union to the world. As couples enter covenant marriages, they serve as a living testimony of who God is, and His glory is magnified. He indicates what He is like through covenant marriages.

Exercising dominion is recognizing where our resources come from and what we should do with them. We are responsible to look after the Earth God entrusts us. God gives resources on this planet at our disposal, and the use of them should be for His glory. Everything belongs to God, but He assigns us to manage resources wisely on His behalf (Psalms 24:1). This includes the things we buy and the materials we make. When resources God gives us are not managed properly, it is like a weed that is hard to pluck out. It can stay rooted for years, causing havoc within the family.

The second is to reproduce by replenishing the earth with godly people by being fruitful and multiplying (Genesis 1:28). We were created with an image and likeness from God that we can pass on to the next generation (Genesis 5:3). Marriage creates an atmosphere of selfless love through human sexual intercourse and the continuation of the human family. The idea here is to establish a legacy of godly descendants. Parents are to protect their children from worldly influence and train them up in the ways of the Lord (Proverbs 22:6). Children do not come with directions, but they do come with instructions. Instructions on training children as soon as they are born come from the Bible. Children are born to parents helpless and with a clean slate for learning. The training of children must be in the direction of righteousness and not the way of the world. Then the children will carry a reflection of God's character to the next generation. God planned for His children who are called for marriage to unite through love for the continuity of His creation. Not all couples will be able to have children. They can be father and mother figures by influencing the next generation of believers through godly integrity.

Lastly is to reign over spiritual attacks against marriage. To reign, couples must operate as a one-flesh union. Intimacy and companionship are sanctified within the confines of marriage to prevent sins of any relationship outside of marriage (Hebrews 13:4). The couple must be stewards of this world and are commanded to have dominion over it by fighting against the dark spiritual forces that are trying to destroy the marriage. The woman was created as a helpmeet to assist the man in navigating the treacherous waters of this fallen world. She is the perfect suitable companion in marriage (Genesis 2:18). From this union, a true oneness in spirit must be agreed upon within the companionship of each other (Amos 3:3). In a covenant marriage, there is no such thing as being independent. Neither spouse is independent of one other (1 Corinthians 11:11). Marriage is a spiritual battle aligned with each other and not against one another. The battle starts from the heart rooted in sin because it is naturally wicked (Jeremiah 17:9). When couples enter marriage, it requires more than hard work. Heart work is the real work guided by the Word of God. Satan is seeking to destroy as many marriages as possible. A strong, godly marriage is offensive to the world that hates God in the first place because it convicts their sinful lifestyles. Each of these enemies wants to steal, kill, and destroy all godly marriages by any means necessary. Once we decide to lose ourselves in Christ, that is where we will find ourselves (Matthew 16:24-25).

Singleness

Singleness is a calling. Like marriage, it is also a gift from God with its benefits. The gifting idea here is for those married must live faithfully with their spouse, and the unmarried should live a celibate lifestyle. People are on different paths when it comes to singleness. These paths include never married, divorced, or widowed. This section will mainly speak to those who are content with never marrying and others who long to be married. Having a significant other is not a requirement to be significant in the eyes of God. When deciding on life-altering decisions, always begin the process with prayer (Psalm 37:4). God has a plan for each of us, and the results will be in His time according to His will. Marriage may or may not happen in this life, but the most important marriage is one with the Lamb for all eternity (Revelation 19:7).

The covenant of singleness is no different than the covenant of marriage. They both take a backseat to the ultimate relationship, which is with Christ. Time is wasted when searching for a life partner without first figuring out your life purpose. The time during the singleness period should be spent on being a bride of Christ before being a groom or a wife. We must keep in mind that not everyone is called to marriage or even promised that whosoever wants marriage will be married. It is possible to live a purposeful life by following Jesus without a spouse. Apostle Paul wrote the following verses that we should embrace singleness if this is part of our gifting:

> But I say this as a concession, not as a commandment. For I wish that all men were even as I myself. But each one has his gift from God, one in this manner and another in that. But I say to the unmarried and the widows: It is good for them if they remain even as I am; but if they cannot exercise self-control, let them marry. For it is better to marry than to burn with passion.
> (1 Corinthians 7:6-9 NKJV)

Paul describes both marriage and singleness as a gift. This gift is for the service of the advancement of the kingdom and should be taken full advantage of. In some ways being single is better than marriage. The unmarried described in these verses are nonvirgins who are divorced or never married. If we desire to not be married, odds are God has called us to singleness. This is a calling devoted to God first, and everything else is secondary. More time can be spent on specific duties on His behalf. This includes abstaining from sexual contact and fully serving God to impact the lives of others for the betterment of the kingdom. This is an ongoing challenge when there is a burning desire to fulfill sexual needs.

We have a choice to live our lives for kingdom purposes or carnal purposes. In other words, we all are given a choice to either live our best life now or to build our life for the afterlife (Matthew 6:33). The problem here is that people often do not see singleness as a gift. They see it as a curse because the waiting period is viewed as a suffering period before getting married. Expectations become unrealistic when we long for a significant other to fix whatever is wrong within us. Disappointment will always happen when we expect someone to fill the void to be whole. It is not biblical to expect a human being to fix our internal issues. According to the following verses, only God can fill all voids and transform us from the inside out:

> For in Him dwells all the fullness of the Godhead bodily; and you are complete in Him, who is the head of all principality and power.
> (Colossians 2:9-10 NKJV)

Marriage does not make us complete, and neither do our significant others. We are complete in Jesus Christ when we receive spiritual circumcision or change in our hearts through His sacrificial death at the cross. No other source is necessary. No longer do we need anyone, human philosophy, or social media to complete us. It is a waste of time searching for worth, value, or significance from anything if Christ already dwells within us. We need to rely on the Lord to fulfill us rather than feeling a need to be married to be whole. That is the great truth from Colossians 2:10. We are a reflection of God's perfection because we are image bearers of Him and wonderfully created by Him (Psalm 139:14). Therefore, we must be connected in a relationship to God first. We must be careful of the longing and placing our focus on spouse, marriage, family, and work, as all of these can be forms of idolatry.

For those who are longing to be married, during this period of singleness God needs us to become whole in Him before we attach to a spouse. We must be prepared for being the right person before marrying the right person. Singleness is the time to have the Holy Spirit improve character by creating a new heart. There may be unresolved pain that needs to be addressed. This could have a negative experience on marriage. God can see our end from the beginning and always knows what is best for each of us. During this time of preparation, life should not be lived in isolation but in a close community and fellowship with believers. The challenge for singles who want to be married is to be distracted from the longings for sexual intimacy, marriage, and family. Therefore, our focus first must be the search for the Master and not a mate.

Social media does not do any favors in posting pictures or videos of weddings, new homes, new babies, and new jobs. It can feel like a popularity contest with the number of followers, subscribers, posts, and likes we have. Some of us are challenged to avoid comparing ourselves to others based on others' social media profiles. This sets the stage for peers who are single and do not have these events in their lives. These virtual experiences can create a secret longing for a relationship or even to replace the people who are posting them. Scrolling, swiping, or clicking posts creates unrealistic expectations and fuels discontentment. We must be mindful that this is an illusion or a snapshot of significant milestones in people. Like Cain, the sin of envy is crouching at the door (Genesis 4:7), but unlike Cain, we cannot allow the Enemy to come in.

Whether we are single or married, we should always give our best for the glory of God (1 Corinthians 10:31). If God calls us to be married; it will take daily work, love, and patience to hold the union together. When it is the season to get married, God will deliver according to His will and glory (Philippians 4:19). The key is how God maneuvers situations where the right person comes along when it is least expected. It is worth noting that God can bring couples together for a purpose that is greater than our understanding. Whatever purpose needs to be fulfilled during the period of singleness, God decides when it is time to change our status. Deviation from His purpose will always result in something less and not God's best for us.

Conclusion

Marriage paints a beautiful picture reflecting Christ as the head and the body of believers as the bride. There is no partnership with Christ, but we must have a submission to Christ (1 Corinthians 11:3). The biggest difference between a covenant and a contractual marriage is that a covenant marriage is where people have Christ as the center of the marriage and a contractual marriage is people are self-managed without Him. A covenant is an agreement we can die from, and a contract is an agreement we can walk away from. Mankind was created with the ability to thrive and enjoy life whether married or not. Many of us will reject the covenant "call" for marriage or singleness. We must learn to be content in whatever season we are in and maximize the circumstances of our lives as a reasonable service to Him (Romans 12:1-2).

Marriage is not a guarantee in this life, but there is an invitation to marriage in the life to come. If we accept the offer of salvation through Jesus Christ, He can give us an abundantly blessed life that may or may not include marriage (John 10:10). Even when setbacks occur while we are doing things God's way by living our lives pleasing to Him, those setbacks are temporary because trials and tribulations happen in this life. This blessed life we are all given may not necessarily be rich, long, or comfortable, but it can be a complete in Christ.

Whether still single or almost married, our legacy is determined by how well we live our lives. Living by biblical principles is the best way to have a secure foundation for a marriage. This will be the second important relationship decision through which the world can witness Christianity in action. The biblical picture of marriage with the husband-and-wife relationship is putting the needs of the marriage ahead of individual needs by serving each other like Christ serves the church. God has given us His instruction manual on how to best honor Him. He has also given us the grace of time with an opportunity to leave a legacy in a relationship intended to be permanent and unbreakable (Matthew 19:5).

Slipping Into Darkness

The Declaration of Independence was an officially signed document on July 4, 1776, specifically designed to choose a form of government and to break free from Great Britain's rule. Part of this document consists of thee well-known phrase "life, liberty and the *pursuit* of *happiness.*" This phrase stands out for all citizens of the United States and is viewed as a core value in this country. However, this document was not originally written for people of color. Black people were slaves, property, and sex objects for the slave owners, used as means of free labor to build wealth for their families and the economy of the United States in its early infancy as a nation. Mexican and Native Americans were slaughtered and forcibly displaced from their lands to meager reservations or forced to live in rural parts of the country.

As far as the United States goes, the Declaration of Independence was followed by the US Constitution and then the Bill of Rights. We should not be surprised that all these were written with divine inspiration from God. After all, He established governments, and we are subjected to the authorities that preside. We live in a country in which many people believe the pursuit of happiness is a right even though it is not a guarantee. Our constitution is signed as the supreme law of the land, but what it declares does not always make it true. The pursuit of happiness can be very tricky because it opens doors to questions. Who or what are we pursuing? In what manner are we to achieve happiness? Like America was breaking free from Great Britain, as humans, we naturally want to break free from God and go our way (Isaiah 53:6).

A popular notion states we can achieve happiness by maximizing pleasure and minimizing pain. We view maximizing relationships through sexual intercourse outside of marriage; however, from God's perspective, this minimizes this type of relationship (1 Corinthians 6:18). We are always lured by our desires to the pleasures of this world that can end in our destruction (James 1:14-15). Sin will always be recycled whenever is the present time because there is nothing new under the sun (Ecclesiastes 1:9). Our sinful nature has us wanting to break free from God and live our lives on our terms—our pursuit of happiness. The three most popular pursuits of happiness in this world are wealth, health, and education.

Happy Wife, Happy Life

This brings us to a popular phrase used by those who do not believe in God and by many who are supposed to believe in God: "Happy wife, happy life." There are books, signs, and stickers encouraging engaged or newly married men to follow this advice as they enter marriage. Some churches have incorporated this idea into their marriage courses and pre-marital conferences. This idea of "happy wife, happy life" is not found in the Scriptures, and pursuing this advice will make *both* husband and wife miserable. It can also lead to the destruction of the marriage. No future husband or wife should ever endorse this idiotic idea.

There was a time when there was a perfect marriage in a perfect world. Eve was seduced by Satan into thinking she was missing out on something and wanted to improve her situation. Adam received firsthand instruction from God but decided to listen to his wife to keep her happy. God gave Adam and Eve everything they needed (Genesis 1:29-30), but Satan tricked them (Genesis 3:16) into thinking happiness is getting everything the heart desires whether it is good or bad. "Happy wife, happy life" gives the impression that after the wedding day, husbands must continue to honor a to-do list and keep their wives happy as a priority. When new and potential husbands make every effort to achieve happiness for their wives, it turns the wife into an idol, and this does not make God happy.

Before marriage, men, in general, will have the natural desire to please their women whether it is during the dating period before the wedding or during the newlywed period after the wedding. After the wedding, it is not the husband's job to make his wife happy. It is unrealistic to believe that this can be done all the time and done right all the time. In any type of relationship, people should never be used for the sole purpose of self-centered fulfillment and personal happiness. Attempting to create happiness for another person has nothing to do with keeping a relationship together in preparation for marriage. No person can be responsible for another's perceived fulfillment in happiness. This approach will overpromise because of high hopes and unreal expectations. It will also underdeliver because satisfaction will never be sustained.

A lasting relationship in a marriage will be built on love, respect, and support by *both* parties. The Scriptures do not instruct a man to make his wife happy. He should be more concerned with pleasing God. Husbands will be held responsible for the spiritual outcome of their families. They must also be able to discern whether advice, wants, and desires from wives are foolish or wise. The Bible gives a clear understanding that it is our holiness and not our happiness that pleases God (1 Peter 1:15-16).

Every person is made in the image of God, and therefore, a wife finds her ultimate meaning, worth, and, happiness in

God alone. God will be unhappy because He is the source of happiness and our search for happiness outside of Him will be turned into an idol. This, of course, breaks the second of the ten commandments (Exodus 20:4). We were made to be complete in God (Colossians 2:10). We must remember that none of us knows our own heart, and if there is one thing we do know, it is that the heart can easily be deceived (Jeremiah 17:9). Eliminate the "happy wife, happy life" catchphrase, and change it to "love the wife, happy life." This will help eliminate this false viewpoint that has been accepted as truth.

Joy vs. Happiness

"Don't Worry Be Happy" is a Grammy award-winning song by Bobby McFerrin released in 1988. The "I just want to be happy" theme is a dangerous one. Happiness always depends on its external factors: people, places, and things. Happiness is overrated because it is a fleeting sentiment that comes in and out of our lives. It disappears quickly when we are suffering or things go bad. Happiness opens the door to the pleasures of this world. It includes intense pleasures in both good and bad things. Some of the good things may be celebrations, birthdays, or anniversaries. It is also possible to be happy in wrong things like pursuing power, prestige, or money. When pursuing happiness as a primary goal of our lives, we are creating the idol of happiness.

Joy, on the other hand, closes that door the same way God closed the door on the Ark with Noah and his family. Joy comes from within love while happiness is on the fringes. In other words, joy is deep, and happiness is shallow. Therefore, joy is undervalued, and happiness is overrated. It is overrated because it cannot be obtained one hundred percent of the time. Happiness is attached to the body, but joy is attached to the soul. Joy always depends on internal factors: trials, tests, and tribulations during the valleys of life. James reminds of the importance of trials and tribulations and how joy is a major factor in the following verses:

> ²My brethren, count it all joy when you fall into
> various trials, ³knowing that the testing of your
> faith produces patience.
> (James 1:2-3 NKJV)

Happiness is a temporary state that comes and goes as circumstances change. Because of imperfections, our future spouse will sometimes let us down and make us feel unhappy. God can offer us joy if we invite Him when we go through trials and tribulation periods to transform us to be better at handling life's conflicts. Our tested faith will allow us to last through any circumstances when the time comes during the marriage. The purpose of marriage is not our happiness but our holiness as a testimony to the world of a representation of Christ. Believers must remember Christ's crucifixion may have been the beginning of weeping, but His resurrection has brought extraordinary joy (Matthew 28:8).

Sexual Revolution

Instead of being fulfilled with the joy found in glorifying God, our hearts, minds, desires, and imaginations can be captured by fleeting moments of pleasure. We are living in a time when the world is turned upside down, calling evil good and good evil (Isaiah 5:20). We are continuing to break the ethical laws of God with our decisions and actions that have an impact on our homes and families, schools, governments, places of worship, courts, and communities. Sex and marriage have become radically separated in modern society. It is now normal for people to sleep together, live together, and even have children together without ever getting married.

God created sex as a wonderful activity. Sex is a gift from God to be enjoyed within the parameters of marriage. This is the most unique earthly relationship among all other relationships. God is the one who created male and female bodies (Genesis

1:27). We are sexual beings, and our bodies are designed in a way to show us enjoying the pleasures of sex. Sexual intercourse was designed by God to be a wonderful experience that promotes love, communication, and intimacy within the confines of marriage. It has its purpose of pleasure, physical intimacy, and procreation. He loves us enough to set the boundaries for it so we will not have to suffer its consequences.

The consequences of sexual encounters are hardly ever considered before the act itself. The consequences are terrible, and the dangers are never appreciated. People cannot deal with the shame of losing virginity, unplanned pregnancy, painful memories, sexual diseases, defiled conscience, and more importantly a loss of fellowship with God. Sexual pleasure only lasts moments. Scripture clearly states that all forms of sex outside of marriage are considered sexually immoral (1 Corinthians 7:2). The consequences of sexual immorality can last years, the rest of your life, or all eternity. This creates unnecessary excess baggage that must be carried into every new relationship.

However, many believe sex before marriage is acceptable. Any behavior can be justified by anyone who refuses to accept what is written in the Bible. Believers have been placed in cultural quicksand when we want to challenge issues of sexual morality. Society has made it difficult to separate believers from the world's influence, especially when only consent and not God's blessing are required in a committed relationship. If two people have consent, then they can do whatever they want. The truth is that it is someone's sinful desire of the heart to engage in premarital sex. What sex was biblically designed for is filtered out to a lesser version acceptable by both believers and nonbelievers. This verse explains the manner in which sex within the confines of marriage must be celebrated:

> [4]Marriage is honorable among all, and the bed undefiled, but fornicators and adulterers God will judge. (Hebrews 13:4 NKJV)

Biblically speaking, no conditions are ever right for unmarried persons to have sex with each other. Our challenge is to serve God at a time when everyone is doing what seems right in their own eyes. All families are fractured in some form or fashion. What sets them apart is which father is holding them together. Which father is setting them apart from the world or keeping them apart from the Kingdom?

Satan twists and distorts the view of sex to add pleasure outside the boundaries God has already established. It is one of his first weapons of choice to bring down a nation from the inside out. He began his assault in the Garden of Eden on the first human family with the question "Has God said?" (Genesis 3:1). The questioning of God's authority continues to this day by rejecting His perfect plan to promote sexual sins outside of marriage.

Premarital sex does not work and never will work because it is habit forming. In most cases, it is not something a couple does once or twice and quits doing. This creates a dependence where there is no real commitment established by both parties. Furthermore, it clouds judgment and makes relationships exceedingly difficult to detach from when one or both parties are not suitable for marriage for whatever reason. The encounter can build a weak foundation in the relationship where communication is disrupted; underlying issues within both people can be covered until it exposed during turbulent times, making them difficult to resolve. Someone can be emotionally attached because of sex and become possessive, which leads to obsession and control. The Bible warns us not to unite our bodies with those who are not our spouses (1 Corinthians 6:16).

Whenever God is removed as final authority and replaced with personal freedoms of sexual expression, all types of chaos will ensue. Most of us are guilty of this, but the Bible does not agree with what we think or feel. Some may believe not having sex before marriage is old fashioned or outdated, but the truth of

God is eternal and will stand forever (1 Peter 1:25). God's Word does not change with culture's opinion on sex (Malachi 3:6) Sex is the most intimate relationship two human beings can have. Sex is ultimately a picture of this redeeming love that God has demonstrated by giving up his Son to save us. Jesus, the Groom, sacrificially gives himself to his beloved bride, the church.

Cohabitation

The sexual revolution from the 1960s in America revived the idea of sexual relations before marriage from Biblical times so that it became a starting point of the decline in marriage and family. Back in the city of Corinth during Biblical times, Apostle Paul addressed the people about the dangers of sexual immorality (1 Corinthians 7:1-3). Culture has shifted the thinking that traditional institutions like marriage are not necessary because they are oppressive, outdated, and do not work. The reasoning here means signing papers and wearing rings is a waste of time.

Since the release of the 2010 census, for the first time in the history of the United States, there are more single people than married people. This means less than half of current households are made up of married couples. The number of Americans who have never married is increasing as well as the number of children born to single parents. The idea of cohabitation is not a modern trend. Now it is part of the dating process that may or may not lead to marriage. Many Christians and churches have bought into it.

Cohabitation is couples living together while having a sexual relationship without being married. Living together in itself is not a sin, but the sexual act makes it a sin. It is not possible to expect commitment in a cohabitation relationship because loyalty is not needed. In other words, there is an expectation of commitment in an uncommitted type of relationship. They would rather be physical than official. Nonmarried women are

pregnant and raising children alone or with significant others.
Men impregnating multiple women and bringing babies into the
world they cannot afford will not take care of them. In this case,
these actions resemble immature teenagers when their hormones
are inflamed and raging out of control. Those who prefer
cohabitation tell God the ways set out by the Bible are too strict,
and we like our way better, as stated in these verses:

> But know this, that in the last days]perilous times will
> come: ²For men will be lovers of themselves, lovers of
> money, boasters, proud, blasphemers, disobedient to
> parents, unthankful, unholy, ³unloving, [b]unforgiving,
> slanderers, without self-control, brutal, despisers
> of good, ⁴traitors, headstrong, haughty, lovers of
> pleasure rather than lovers of God, ⁵having a form
> of godliness but denying its power. And from such
> people turn away! (2 Timothy 3:1-5NKJV)

People still want to be married, but careers, goals, and other
ambitions are driving them to put it off later. Not everyone will
want God. For those who do want Him, it must be done on
their terms. We believe in engaging in sexual acts now and are
not concerned about marriage later. Many will choose to live
together and learn all the habits before deciding if marriage is
the next step. Some believe other options are available when
relationships do not work out. However, this gives an illusion of
"plenty of fish in the sea" or opportunities to find new partners.
During the dating process, we come up with this brilliant
plan by sharing our bodies sexually until we are comfortable
in finding the right one. This is done by both believers and
nonbelievers alike. Now more than ever Christian behaviors are
hardly distinguishable from unbelievers in the world today.

One of many curses since the Fall is mankind's arrogant
confidence in our thinking. Many are rebelling by reinterpreting
what the Bible says to approve whatever sinful actions chosen in

their lives. The fact that cohabitation is common does not mean it is normal. Animals exist on instinct, and they do not have a moral compass like humans. They mate and reproduce without reasoning or thinking. We are made in the image of God, and we are more than exchanging bodily fluids for pleasure. Our bodies have a dignity that needs to be recognized and respected. We should want to make a serious commitment in relationships that lead to marriage.

The Lord does not lead couples to live together before marriage. Couples selfishly do that on their own when they believe they are right in their own eyes by living together and engaging in sex before marriage (Proverbs 21:2). Men and women are meant to come together in marriage. It is the commitment of "becoming one" that God blesses. Key principles in marriage are already outlined earlier in this book (Genesis 2:24).

Sin is the enemy of every relationship. Selfishness is the driving force that creates a wedge between potential husband and wife. As soon as one party feels or believes needs are not met, then there will be conflict. The blessing is in the giving and not the receiving. (Acts 20:35). Even Jesus confronted a Samaritan woman at the well in John chapter 4. He revealed something significant that we often miss in this passage. In verses 13 through 18, Jesus says to her:

> 13Jesus answered and said to her, "Whoever drinks of this water will thirst again, 14but whoever drinks of the water that I shall give him will never thirst. But the water that I shall give him will become in him a fountain of water springing up into everlasting life." 15The woman said to Him, "Sir, give me this water, that I may not thirst, nor come here to draw." 16Jesus said to her, "Go, call your husband, and come here." 17The woman answered and said, "I

have no husband." Jesus said to her, "You have
well said, 'I have no husband,' ¹⁸for you have had
five husbands, and the one whom you now have is
not your husband; in that, you spoke truly."
(John 4:13-18 NKJV)

The result is the offer of eternal life, but what sin was the woman committing? The woman had been hiding the fact that the man she was living with was not her husband. She was living in adultery with all those former husbands. Jesus showed that living together and marriage are not the same thing. Jesus also showed that just because someone calls a relationship marriage, it does not mean that Jesus considers it marriage. As we can see from this passage, cohabitation is not a modern trend. There is nothing new under the sun (Ecclesiastes 1:9).

Electronic media are loudly promoting cohabitation in movies, videos, and many other outlets. Churches, unfortunately, are quite silent on this matter because many of the congregants are living this lifestyle. Sadly, many Christians have adopted many of today's secular values as their own. They embrace convenience at any cost—sex without rules, companionship without commitment, and relationship without responsibility. Cohabitation reverses this order of marriage and then becomes one or eliminates the marriage component. Cohabitation is also a direct rejection of God's ways and robs His glory by not showing the image of Christ and the church as a testimony of the relationship. God does not reward the disobedient, especially those who are purposefully and continually living against His commands (1 John 3:6). We cannot expect God to bless us when we willfully choose to disobey Him by living with and engaging in sexual relations with someone we are not married to much like as parents, we withhold blessings from our children when they willfully rebel or are disobedient against us.

Divorce

Over the last 50 years, the social stigma surrounding divorce has lost its luster. At one time it was difficult to obtain a divorce, but today this is a common occurrence. We may know someone who had a divorce or grew up as a child with divorced parents. Someone somewhere is filing divorce papers at the courthouse. Standards have become relaxed concerning divorce, not only in our governmental institutions but in our churches as well. When standards concerning marriage land outside of Scripture, we can expect the destruction of the relationship.

Couples who are planning for marriage must be aware of reducing the risks of divorce. They will believe when they walk down the aisle their marriage will last forever. Couples will believe other people will have problems and never experience the heartache of divorce. Unfortunately, marriage is problematic all over the landscape when at least half of them will end in divorce. According to the Bible, God is not a fan of divorce (1 Corinthians 7:10-11).

No relationship comes with a guarantee. The roles of husband and wife once complemented one another, but now, in most cases, have confused one another. Even if men and women grew up in a two-parent Christian household, they are still at risk for divorce because of the human heart (Jeremiah 17:9). The marriage will collapse because the heart of selflessness changes to selfishness along with an unwillingness to forgive between the couple. When pride removes God from the throne of the relationship, the marriage will unravel very quickly in the direction of divorce. Even the believer is not immune to the possibility of divorce.

In every relationship, there are storms and conflicts within the relationship. When times become difficult, we want to give up and quit. Things like domestic abuse, addiction, and adultery come to mind as dealbreakers. In most marriages, however, when each of us was at our worst, God still loved us and did not leave us. Divorce should be the last resort and not the first response.

Throughout the Bible, the Pharisees were not interested in Jesus's ministry. They were not willing to convert to the Truth and gain salvation through Jesus. They wanted to overthrow Him by any means necessary because He was a threat to their way of life. They set traps to get Jesus to contradict what is written in Scripture. In the following verses, the Pharisees thought they were able to trap Jesus politically and theologically on the topic of divorce:

> [3]Some Pharisees came to him to test him. They asked, "Is it lawful for a man to divorce his wife for any and every reason?" [4]"Haven't you read," he replied, "that at the beginning the Creator 'made them male and female,' [5]and said, 'For this reason, a man will leave his father and mother and be united to his wife, and the two will become one flesh? [6]So they are no longer two, but one flesh. Therefore, what God has joined together, let no one separate." [7]"Why then," they asked, "did Moses command that a man give his wife a certificate of divorce and send her away?" [8]Jesus replied, "Moses permitted you to divorce your wives because your hearts were hard. But it was not this way from the beginning. [9]I tell you that anyone who divorces his wife, except for sexual immorality, and marries another woman commits adultery."
> (Matthew 19: 3-9 NKJV)

When considering marriage, understand the importance of getting to the heart of any conflict through effective communication. Sin will always find a crack in marriages to rupture it over time until it is fully destroyed, like little foxes spoiling the vineyard (Song of Solomon 2:15). This happens when the needs of both husband and wife are unmet and not addressed. Husbands are not loving their wives while leading sacrificially and wives are not respecting their husbands by supporting with cooperation. As much grace as God has given us when we sin against Him daily, couples should give the same amount of grace to each other during the time of marriage.

The Bible does give two acceptable reasons for divorce. The first is the abandonment of a Christian by an unbelieving spouse (1 Corinthians 7:15), and the second is sexual immorality, which includes adultery (Matthew 5:32). Both instances can be forgiven, reconciled, and restored. Divorce in these examples is an allowance and not a requirement. The mindset of a couple entering marriage is to have divorce-proof expectations by considering God's perspective. Of course, this is much more difficult than it sounds.

Conclusion

We should not be surprised by moral bankruptcy around the world because God is not. God saw this coming because he is the Alpha and the Omega, able to see the beginning and end of time (Revelation 22:13). Satan's goal is to destroy everything God has created and to put himself in God s place. However, he is sadly mistaken because he is a dead creature walking, and the Creator will ultimately destroy his creation. Ecclesiastes 1:9 reminds us that "there is nothing new under the sun" (All the sins being done now have already been done). This is exactly like turning the clock back to the pre-flood period in the days of Noah.

Everything about sex, marriage, and relationships is a perversion of its original version, and the United States will never be the same from this point forward. The concept of the nuclear family is rejected because the world hates God and His perfect plan. The goal is to destroy and redefine what the Bible says about God's perfect design of sexuality through marriage and family.

Our default nature is to do everything opposite from God until we are corrected.

Christians are called for a different standard of living than the rest of humanity. The challenge right now is serving God at a time when everyone is living what seems right in their own eyes. Our walk must be after the spirit and not after the flesh (Romans 8:1). This is a narrow kind of walk that is more difficult to attain. God's principles and guidelines from Scripture never change. If something was true over two thousand years ago, then it is still true today. These teachings are as valid today as ever and are superior to anything devised by mankind. To follow them gives honor in our lives and glory to Him. God's way gives us the best opportunity for happiness with His hand of protection. We are to be new creatures as our old ways must pass away (2 Corinthians 5:17).

Sexual sins, cohabitation, and divorce are forgivable sins, and God is more than able to forgive us of all our sins. He is more than willing to forgive us of all lust and free us from all impurity through the cleansing blood of his Son, Jesus (1 John 1:9). Turn away from all sexual immorality and seek to live under God's gracious and forgiving love. Understanding that we are complete in Christ by faith through grace is one of the most basic truths of the Christian faith (Ephesians 2:8-9). We do not have to sin or be deceived by the philosophies of the world. Jesus set the stage for saying the last sayings on the cross before he died. What will be your seven last words you hear after you die? Will they be "I never knew you: depart from me" (Matthew 7:23) or "well done, thou good and faithful servant" (Matthew 25:21). The choice is ours.

Final Remarks

Our existence has an unchanging God in an ever-changing world. Not everyone will receive the truth or care for it. God's truth in his design for marriage remains unchanged despite any recent or future changes in policies or law. Our opinions and resolutions do not alter what is written in the Bible. God's Word has already said what we sow to the flesh we will reap in the destruction (Galatians 6:8). Yet we are reminded to speak the truth in love and not beat people over the head with Scripture (Ephesians 4:15). Pre-marital relationships in themselves are not sinful; what the people involved do in those relationships determines if they are sinful.

Entertainment programming has professional writers to make lines sound so romantic. Yet they are usually void of Biblical foundation. So many reality shows on dating and marriage give viewers a chance to be "hooked" on bad behavior by the worst humanity has to offer. People who are willing to portray themselves as villains bring fame and notoriety to themselves. This brings instant ratings to the program to prevent viewers from boredom. These fantasies have warped the viewer's minds about what the institution of marriage is supposed to be like. This influences viewers to live out the way people are living through media. Believers must be aware the media in some of their programs will sprinkle just enough good to cover their evil agenda, confusing what is right as wrong and what is wrong as right (Isaiah 5:20).

Wife, Life, and Legacy recaptures the minds of those of the pre-marriage period of their lives. Principles and guidelines that can help prevent marital destruction are outlined in this book. Does this mean couples who are within marriage will never divorce? Of course not, but this book gives a marriage a far better chance of success depending on how sin is handled and how often forgiveness is utilized in the relationship. Love wins when marriages go the distance God's way as written in the Scriptures. There is a war against marriage and the nuclear family, and all of us are on the frontlines.

Our modern-day dysfunction in families should not surprise us. Women like to blame men who don't step up or put effort into pursuing anymore. Men willfully and cowardly walk away from their purpose as the spiritual leader in marriage and family (1 Corinthians 11:3). Men like to blame women, saying they feel like they compete with each other rather than working together. Women are forced into the headship role God did not create them for. After all, Isaiah prophesized that in the last days women would be ruling the homes, children oppressing society, and people openly rebelling against God while parading their sins without shame (Isaiah 3:5,9-12).

Most psychologists and sociologists know when marriage began, but they reject God as its perfect designer. Many of these people may have good intentions but often use references other than the Bible. They only see the history of human evolution through some explosion theory and are leading the cause by voicing their opinions against traditional families and marriage. New legislation may be passed or laws amended, but the Word of God is unchanging. Whoever we love does not change God's rules. Long after we are gone, His Word will stand forever (Isaiah 40:8).

Wife, Life, and Legacy has nothing to do with opinion, male ego, toxic masculinity, or male chauvinism, but everything to do with the principles given in Scripture that allow each role to complement. Times change, but truth does not. Biblical truth is universal and eternal. It has always been countercultural. It surpasses man's truth, which shifts like sinking sand. Unfortunately, many professing Christians are going to this extreme today, excusing their sin because they do not feel it is wrong, even when the Bible says it is.

It never ceases to amaze how sin is reused and named something else like it never existed before. No matter what is considered a new thought, there is nothing new under the sun (Ecclesiastes 1:9). This means sin is portrayed differently and using different terminology. Nevertheless, God is still sovereign and sits on the throne, supervising the affairs of mankind. There is no good thing that will be withheld from us if we are His children (Psalm 84:11). Even Christians have lost their influence on society by compromising their beliefs and catering to the culture.

We do not have the right to remain silent. The church has been silent for too long and failed to stand up for the biblical view of marriage. When it is not preached in pulpits, it is even worse. Male-female roles in marriage are in chaos because the church is losing ground to the culture. We are brainwashed, and we allow society to promote "accepting" everyone and everything. If someone's actions do not fit our standards, then we are "judging" that person and not being "open-minded" enough. People are also taught that they must accept everything that is considered inclusive and tolerant—except Christianity. When we depart from or fail to stand up for the biblical view of marriage, we are taking a step away from the gospel itself. Any threat of godlessness anywhere is a threat of godlessness everywhere.

Wife, Life, and Legacy is designed to squash excuses or fears by stepping out on faith and allowing God to step into our relationships. Some of these fears of relationships leading to marriage are well documented with the top three questions for all couples: Are we marrying the right person? Will we lose our identity? Will our marriage end in divorce? Our perception can paralyze us in acting on what is right without operating in faith in Christ who will reveal in His time. Fear tends to make us objectify our parents in relationships, especially if abuse, divorce, or separation is involved while growing up. Some ideas are so ingrained into your consciousness that it takes God, faith, and a whole lot of courage to go against an upbringing and experience. We should never judge the future of marital relationships based on our parents' past or current situation.

Joshua told the Israelites to choose this day whom they will serve (Joshua 24:15). As in Joshua's day, it is true for us today that all it takes is one generation to forget God along with the teachings and principles outlined in the Bible. We cannot continue to go along to get along with the destructive trends in our culture. A thriving nation with its foundational principles depends on standards set by families. Even if parents are Christian, that does not mean the children will follow suit and become Christian. Current trends suggest children beginning at the age of eighteen are leaving the faith in droves. Every major empire has fallen because of decaying moral and sexual standards, especially within the traditional family unit.

The Epitome of Love Recap

Love is the greatest virtue and the most difficult concept to grasp in human experience. It is a commitment to give up everything for someone else—great ideas, career opportunities, romance, warm fuzzy feelings, or butterflies in the stomach. None of these things are considered love. Love is a choice we make based on the act of the will of our hearts. It gives us the greatest feeling on one hand and the greatest pain on the other.

In the love chapter of 1 Corinthians 13, the Corinthian church was using their spiritual gifts apart from love. Paul makes the point that the use of their God-given gifts will be useless if the Corinthians do not make love their priority. We should notice the virtue of patience—not perfection—is the first item listed in the blueprint of love in 1 Corinthians 13:4-7. Patience creates perseverance and fuels glorifying marriages in the sight of God. It gives a perfect illustration of marriage with God as Bridegroom by His longsuffering patience with us as the bride.

Human love, however, is imperfect for without God there are no conditions to love by extending grace. Because of sin, there will always be a continual conflict between men and women when they place their self-interest above the other (Genesis 3:16). Not only does God's grace cover a multitude of our sins, but it also eliminates the need for perfection in relationships, which does not exist anyway (1 Peter 4:8). According to the following verse, our relationship with Jesus Christ is very important:

> If you love Me keep My commandments.
> (John 14:15)

Love does not love without obedience to the Word. *Love and obedience cannot be separated because they go together and* show how much we love. The love we have for others and the faith we have in Christ prove our obedience to His commandments. God's love is for everyone in the world who believes in Him (John 3:16).

The problem with the term *unconditional love* is that people are not afraid of God. There is this picture that God loves everybody, and everybody will be saved. This false definition of love uses words such as *tolerant, inclusion,* or *diversity* while leaving out accountability from the darkness of sin with self-destructive behaviors. They only see Him as a God of love full of grace and mercy, but He is also a God of wrath, and He will show it when He determines that it is necessary. To sum up, God's love is unconditional to the entire world with no one excluded. At the same time, to receive eternal life, His love is conditional to those who by faith accept Jesus as Lord and Savior.

Building Boaz Recap

Biblical manhood is the starting point of a legacy that matters for a master to answer. All of us serve a master, and denying this will not change the truth. Either we serve sin or obedience (Romans 6:16). The mission with a vision is the life purpose in the journey, writing daily events through every decision made. A farsighted vision that recognizes the importance of how passing the word down is crucial to living out tomorrow (Psalm 145:4) must be attached to the mission. A mate to cultivate is a man who is prepared to cherish his soon-to-be wife above everyone else. Such a man is knowledgeable of the word and accepts guidance from the Holy Spirit.

God placed full responsibility for the family on the shoulders of husbands. They must serve as godly kings, providers, and protectors. This resembles the role of Christ as the bridegroom and the church as the bride through sacrificial love (Ephesians 5:25). An effective spiritual leader honors the Lord and always attempts to do what is right as defined in the Bible.

The key to a great marital life and blessed children is choosing the right godly mate from the very beginning. The wife that is chosen solidifies what kind of legacy is left behind for generations to come. Men should never marry for beauty and good looks alone without examining the character inside. A Hell or Heaven kind of marriage is determined by this second-most important choice that can be made. True toxic masculinity is passiveness by neglecting the role of leadership.

Legacy is leaving the truth about God from one generation to the next one. We are encouraged to leave an inheritance to our children and grandchildren (Proverbs 13:22). They are the eyes and ears of tomorrow in a time their parents will not see. Material possessions left for the family are good to live with, but they will never have eternal value. Our children and grandchildren should be able to share stories with families of faith in God. Every man must examine within himself what kind of legacy is being left to the next generation.

Ruth Ready Recap

Solomon knew a bad wife is worse than being alone and she is more bitter than death (Ecclesiastes 7:26). He should have known this after failing one thousand times in choosing the right woman as his bride (1 Kings 11:1-6). Ruth ready is biblical womanhood that all Christian women should live by whether single, married, mothers, or childless. Part of being Ruth ready is being the right choice as a bride. When she is being a wife before becoming a wife, she must be significant to magnificent, soft at all costs, and supportive and cooperative.

Biblical womanhood has everything to do with your posture of heart, surrendered and submitted to God with reverence for Him. The role of wife and mother is secondary compared to being the daughter of the King. Once she discovers the ways she can display Christ's glory and the gospel's beauty in every area of her life, then she is ready to be a wife. A legacy maker is a suitable choice for a wife who serves as a helpmeet and hard worker, honorable and hospitable. This resembles the role of the Bride for Christ through sacrificial submission.

Christians and non-Christians alike have come to think of submission as oppressive. There is a failure to see the greatness of submission in the Kingdom of God. Jesus Himself submits to the will of the Father by doing His work. So, while God places the bulk of family responsibility upon the husband, He places a lighter burden upon the wife and instructs her to submit to her husband's leadership, as the husband submits to Christ in all things (Ephesians 5:22–24). Wives are at their best when they are submissive while being protected, cherished, and provided for. True happiness for a prospective wife will come from her love for God and willingly accepting her role. It will not come from her career or her independence.

Before I Do Recap

In biblical times, the process of meeting a spouse had very little to do with compatibility and personality traits and everything to do with family lineage and economic status. The term *dating* did not exist in biblical times, and many places in our world today do not practice what we call modern dating either. There was a comparison between the terms *modern dating* and *Christian dating*. Modern dating uses our feelings as a guide with expectations of sexual involvement and no expectations of marriage to find someone. Christian dating is using the Bible as a guide with no expectations of sexual involvement and expectations of marriage.

As building a solid foundation is necessary for Christian dating, these core components must be present before any marriage beings. Character is an objective set of moral standards that align with Scripture. Communication fosters trust and commitment with no hidden agendas. Community is like a warm circle surrounded by a godly council of family members, mentors, and close friends. Commitment requires a connection through intimacy that honors Christ no matter the circumstances. Composition means understanding the unique roles that God has set for both men and women. Cash Management is properly handling spending and budgeting along with merging assets and debts. Children must be discussed—how many, how to raise, and how to discipline them in the ways of the Lord.

There are no clear-cut answers found in the Bible as to how long the dating period should be before marriage. Christian dating, unlike modern dating, is not meant to be conducted over many years. It is meant to be a brief time to see if the couple is suitable for marriage. Finding the right person usually lasts six months but does not go beyond two years. When choosing a spouse, if their relationship draws us closer to sin than salvation in Christ, then we are wasting our time.

Covenant or Contract Recap

For any couple considering marriage, there are important differences between a modern-day contract and a biblical covenant. Contract marriage focuses on a worldview mindset that overrides a biblical one. This type of marriage is based on fear or distrust, where either party can walk away at any time. Contract marriages are considered temporary, with a time limit that can be altered if the conditions of the marriage change. This means a divorce is an option when someone is not happy. When this happens, it comes with financial consequences. God is not active in this marriage (Exodus 20:3). There is also the idea that marriage is nothing more than a piece of paper issued by the state.

Covenant marriage was instituted by God himself by reflecting His image, reigning through dominion, and reproducing children for the next generation. Marriage is a covenant set by God between two people, a man and a woman united until death parts the union. They are no longer two separate and independent bodies but united as one flesh. Consequently, they become one in everything. This includes in-laws and extended families. God also designed marriage but set specific structures with it. Husbands and wives are equal in worth but unequal in roles within the family.

Singleness is not a death sentence but a gift. Although, there are currently more single people than married people, it boils down to finding the right person. In some ways, singleness is better than marriage, but it is treated as a curse instead of a blessing. The pursuit of searching for the perfect person who does not exist is useless. The right person will be the one that will be the perfect fit. No man or woman completes us; only God can fill any void.

What I have learned about staying married for over twenty-six years is marriage is like a job, and work must be put in 24 hours a day, 7 days a week, 365 days a year. The biggest key to the longevity of marriage is for two imperfect people to be willing to forgive each other and love each other every day (Colossians 3:12-14). This might be easy to say, but it's hard to do. In this life, nothing worth having doesn't take work.

God must be allowed to be the foundation of the marriage. Knowing He exists is one thing, but knowing him personally is quite another. The Bible has sixty-six books, over forty authors, and one story. This instruction manual outlasts any philosophical, sociological, and psychological thinking because it will stand forever (Isaiah 40:8). It must be opened, read, interpreted correctly, and applied to get to personally know Him. Without Scripture, prayer, and worship, there is no way the marriage will function properly.

Slipping into Darkness Recap

Sin is always evolving and changing its name with the times, but in essence, its name outlined in the Bible is still the same. Society is whispering to us that we deserve whatever we want. When we make the other person an idol, we are consuming them and the ways of the world at the same time. In that process, we are pushing God aside. Our culture blesses our actions; it is so easy to live our lives apart from God. Whenever we devote our lives to pursuing wealth, education, and health, we will never be satisfied (James 4:1-2).

The Biblical route in relationships for many is considered boring or too traditional. Fools believe marriage is just a piece of paper and love is all that is needed to justify sins by engaging in sexual activity before marriage. Cohabitation expects commitment in an uncommitted type of relationship. Sex outside of marriage is inevitable when couples move in together. This is considered an important part of the modern dating experience for some believers. Some Christians even believe it is ok to "carry before we marry." In other words, there is nothing wrong with bringing children into the world outside the confines of marriage. This is the creature telling the Creator, "Your way of following rules outlined in this Bible is boring. I want to do things my way. I am missing out on the fun, and I would appreciate it if you either look the other way or leave me alone."

Paul discusses the sinfulness of all sexual relations outside of marriage. According to Scripture, it is the only sin against one's own body (1 Corinthians 6:18). God has set the standard in His word for how we approach Him with our bodies *before* marriage. Sexual intercourse was created by God with clear boundaries, but our greatest enemies—the world, our flesh, and Satan—want us to remove those boundaries. Cohabitation embraces the "trying before buying" way of dating. This leads to an ungodly way of living before marriage, such as sex without rules, companionship without commitment, and a relationship without responsibility. We would rather be physical than official.

In the case of divorce, it would not be necessary if husbands love their wives and wives are respectful to their husbands (Ephesians 5:33). The Bible is a better teacher than experience; Scriptures have us learn and live rather than live and learn. We must teach our children or young adults about some of the mistakes we made in our youth. When mistakes are made, forget the excuses as to why because they do not change reality and the consequences will still follow. God cannot bless sin in any form. He will not bless relationships that go against His clearly expressed will (Romans 1:26-27). Christians have a higher calling than living like the rest of humanity. Remember, champions wear rings and hold titles.

Conclusion

Wife, Life, and Legacy reminds us that our legacy begins with selecting and accepting spouses who are right for us. God is always primary, and the relationship is secondary. The only legacy that truly matters through marriage is the hearts that are written with the belief that Jesus Christ is Lord and Savior. The heart is the starting point. Then it must be taught to our children, and our children must teach their children and so on (Deuteronomy 6:6-8). This is how we have a real *future for our children.* When this example is displayed at home, children of these unions and other witnesses will build lineages that will have a lasting effect for generations and generations.

When we think of leaving a legacy for our family, we often think about leaving behind a monetary inheritance of wealth. The Bible does not disagree with this principle (Proverbs 13:22). The legacy left by us must focus on the next life as well as the one life we are given. One day we will all stand before Him to give an account of every thought, word, or deed during our lifetime. As someone's future ancestors, we must have the mindset of leaving a legacy that continues for eternity.

Christ left the ultimate legacy for all of us. He lived a sinless life and died for us while we were yet sinners (Romans 5:8). Even when we rejected, rebelled, and reviled by putting Jesus on the cross, it is still no comparison to His crucifixion, death, and resurrection out of His love for us. His selfless act on the cross is the life that leaves a legacy of riches and promises of the Kingdom that are within reach for all who believe and trust Him with their lives. The legacy we leave is the life we live through the life of Christ by the power of the Holy Spirit. It is His legacy reflecting through us for the blessing of our families and others. Jesus is our perfect example of the life we should live.

The Bible begins with the creation of man and woman in the Garden of Eden united for marriage (Genesis 2) and ends with the "wedding feast between Christ and His Church" (Revelation 19:7-9 21:1-2). We make our vows and anticipate the coming marriage supper of the Lamb. This means getting our souls ready for the afterlife with our eternal union with Jesus. When it comes to preparation for marriage, men should rely on God by trusting in Him that He will guide them in their divine rightful position as the sacrificial, loving leaders they were meant to be. Women must love God first, be virtuous, and be willing to be led by exchanging their independence for dependence on God alone before saying the words "I do."

Suggested References

https://blackdemographics.com/.

https://www.merriam-webster.com/dictionary/marriage.

English Standard Version, Bible Gateway. www.biblegateway.com.

New King James Version, Bible Gateway, www.biblegateway.com.

Arceneaux, Kitty. 2019. *While You Are Waiting on Your Boaz, You Better Be Ruth Ready*. Independently published.

Ballenger, Mark. 2018. "Love Is More Than a Sacrificial Choice." *Apply God's Word* (July 1). http://applygodsword.com/love-is-more-than-a-choice/.

Blackburn, Lindsay. 2011. "Modern Day Boaz." Startmarriageright.com. September 20. http://www.startmarriageright.com/2011/09/a-modern-day-boaz/

Babgan, Martin, and Deidre Babgan. 1997. "Unconditional Love & Acceptance." *Psychoheresy Awareness Letter* 5 (5). http://www.psychoheresy-aware.org/unconlov.html.

Baucham, Voddie Jr. 2009. *What He Must Be…If He Wants to Marry My Daughter*. Wheaton, IL: Crossway Publishing.

Brown, Aaron. 2021. "Why Sex is About More Than Just Consent." Crosswalk. November 19. https://www.crosswalk.com/faith/spiritual-life/why-sex-is-about-more-than-just-consent.html

Brown, T. D. 2013. *"I Don't Need a Man": Think like a Godly Man, Act Like a Virtuous Woman*. Maitland, FL: Xulon Press.

Bricker, Sophia. 2022. "How Should Christians Approach Dating?" Christianity.com. August 18. https://www.christianity.com/wiki/christian-life/how-should-christians-approach-dating.html.

Britton, Katherine. 2022. "Dancing Backwards." Crosswalk. March 24. https://www.crosswalk.com/devotionals/crosswalk-devo/crosswalk-the-devotional-feb-25-2009-11600006.html.

Brotman, Barbara. 2000. "To Love, Honor, and Obey." *Chicago Tribune* (September 27). www.chicagotribune.com/news/ct-xpm-2000-09-27-0009270346-story.html

Bucknell, Paul J. 2019. "Creating a Godly Legacy." BFF. May 25. https://bffbible.org/marriage/view/creating-a-godly-legacy.

Carr, Steve. 2007. "What Is God's Design and Calling for You as a Husband?" Covenant Keepers. *https://covenantkeepers.org/what-is-god-s-design-and-calling-for-you-as-a-husband.*

Chappell, Brian. 2000. "Alpha Male Meets Alpha and Omega." *World Magazine* (May 20). https://world.wng.org/2000/05/alpha_male_meets_alpha_and_omega.

Clarke, Brian. 2015. "Religious Marriage vs. Legal Marriage." The Faculty Lounge. September. www.thefacultylounge.org/2015/09/religious-marriage-v-legal-marriage.html.

Creech, R. Robert. 2013. "What Is a Christian Marriage?" Explore God. https://www.exploregod.com/articles/what-is-christian-marriage

Daly, Jim. 2013. "Is Online Dating Biblical?" *Focus on the Family* (May 29). https://jimdaly.focusonthefamily.com/is-online-dating-biblical/.

Fairchild, Mary. 2020. "Christian Wedding Symbols: The Meaning Behind the Traditions." Learn Religions. June 13. *https://www.learnreligions.com/christian-wedding-traditions-701948.*

Gola, Stephen. 2006. "God's Unconditional Love: It's Moral, It's Conditional." Divorce Hope. http://www.divorcehope.com/pdf/love_its_moral_its_conditional.pdf.

Grunor, Mark. 2008. "A Husband's Greatest Need: Respect." Crosswalk. November 3. https://www.crosswalk.com/family/marriage/a-husbands-greatest-need-respect-11590402.html.

DeRamus, Dwight E. Jr. 2017. *Disappearing Dads.* Lansing, IL: Trey Nickel Publishing, 22–25.

DeRamus, Dwight E. Jr. 2017. *Disappearing Dads.* Lansing, IL: Trey Nickel Publishing, 54–55.

Flurry, Gerald. 1999. "Conspiracy Against Fatherhood." *The Trumpet* (September). https://www.thetrumpet.com/323-conspiracy-against-fatherhood.

Flurry, Gerald, and Joel Hilliker. 2009. "The War Against Family." *The Trumpet* (September). https://www.thetrumpet.com/6365-the-war-against-family.

Harris, Janelle. 2016. "Pastors Tell Black Women to be Passive and Wait for Love. I Don't Believe in That." *The Washington Post* (November 25). https://www.washingtonpost.com/news/soloish/

wp/2016/11/03/pastors-tell-black-women-to-be-passive-and-wait-for-love-i-dont-believe-in-that/.

Hilliker, Joel. 2017. "What Does It Mean to Be a Man?" *The Trumpet* (May–June). https://www.thetrumpet.com/15656-what-does-it-mean-to-be-a-man.

Hopler, Whitney. 2008. "The Differences Between Men's and Women's Brains." Crosswalk. February 21. https://www.crosswalk.com/family/marriage/the-differences-between-mens-and-womens-brains-11568752.html.

Hopson, Judi L., Hopson, Emma H. Hagen, Ted. 2018. "Person to Person: Why Men Need Nurturing by Women." *Chicago Tribune*. November 19. https://www.chicagotribune.com/lifestyles/sns-tns-bc-self-person-to-person-20181119-story.html

Jonel, Aleccia. 2013. "'The New Normal': Cohabitation on the Rise, Study Finds." NBC News. April 4. https://www.nbcnews.com/healthmain/new-normal-cohabitation-rise-study-finds-1C9208429.

Jones, Erik. 2014. "Why Real Men are Becoming Extinct?" Life Hope and Truth. June 9. https://lifehopeandtruth.com/relationships/blog/why-real-men-are-becoming-extinct/.

Kostenberger, Andereas. 2011. "The Bible's Teaching on Marriage and Family." *Family Research Council*. p..4-7. https://downloads.frc.org/EF/EF11J34.pdf.

Kramer, Stephanie. 2019. "U.S. has World's Highest Rate of Children Living in Single-Parent Households." Pew Research Center. December 12. https://www.pewresearch.org/fact-tank/2019/12/12/u-s-children-more-likely-than-children-in-other-countries-to-live-with-just-one-parent/.

Larimore, Walt. 2016. "Husbands and Wives are Hardwired to Complement Each Other." Focus on the Family. November 15. https://www.focusonthefamily.com/marriage/husbands-and-wives-are-hardwired-to-complement-each-other/.

Lindsey, Joel. 2015. "Marriage Covenant vs. Contract." FTC. October 20. https://ftc.co/blog/posts/marriage-covenant-vs-contract.

Logan, Cally. 2021. "What Does the Bible Say About Dating?" Crosswalk. June 15. https://www.crosswalk.com/family/singles/what-does-the-bible-say-about-dating.html.

Mahoney, Kelli. 2019. "Bible Verses on Unconditional Love." Learn Religions. August 22. https://www.learnreligions.com/bible-verses-on-unconditional-love-712135.

Massey, Emily. 2022. "What is Courting and How is it Different from Dating?" I Believe. January 20. https://www.ibelieve.com/relationships/what-is-courting-how-is-it-different-from-dating.html.

McLeroy, Leigh. 2013. "Is God's Love Unconditional?" Explore God. https://www.exploregod.com/articles/is-gods-love-unconditional.

Mohler, Albert Jr. 2005. "From Boy to Man—The Marks of Manhood." Albert Mohler. April 21. https://albertmohler.com/2005/04/21/from-boy-to-man-the-marks-of-manhood-part-one.

Muir, Caitlin. 2013. "What are the Real Red Flags in Dating?" Relevant Magazine. January 31. https://relevantmagazine.com/life5/relationships/what-are-real-red-flags-dating/.

Neffinger, Veronica. 2017. "What Does Many are Called but Few are Chosen Actually Mean? Crosswalk. June 9. https://

www.crosswalk.com/blogs/christian-trends/what-does-many-are-called-but-few-are-chosen-actually-mean.html.

Nevils, Noah. 2019. "What are the 4 Types of Love in the Bible." Bible Reasons. March 31. https://biblereasons.com/what-are-the-4-types-of-love-in-the-bible/.

Pride, Víctor 2012. "How to Pick the Right Wife." Bold and Determined. January 21. https://boldanddetermined.com/pick-the-right-wife/.

Reid, John O. 2016. "Ready Answer." *Forerunner*. March–April. https://www.cgg.org/index.cfm/fuseaction/Library.sr/CT/RA/k/1703/Many-Are-Called-Few-Are-Chosen.htm.

Rice Judy. 2015. "What's Love Got to Do With It? Defying the Love is Love Movement." Clash Daily. July 4. https://clashdaily.com/2015/07/whats-love-got-to-do-with-it-defying-the-love-is-love-movement/.

Stelzer, Becky. 2007. "Inferior or Equal." *Answers Magazine*. January 1. https://answersingenesis.org/family/gender/inferior-or-equal/.

Strauss, Richard L. 2004. "But the Greatest of These." Bible.org. June 28. https://bible.org/seriespage/6-greatest-these.

Solomon, Larry. 2015. "Does the Bible Teach Happy Wife, Happy Life." Biblical Gender Roles. June 23. https://biblicalgenderroles.com/2015/06/23/does-the-bible-teach-happy-wife-happy-life-2/.

Synder, Howard A. 1995. "Is God's Love Unconditional?" *Christianity Today*. July 17. https://www.christianitytoday.com/ct/1995/july17/is-gods-love-unconditional.html.

Torrance, Katara. 2019. "10 Ways You Can Be a Better Help-meet." Medium. September 26. https://mshelpmeet.medium.com/10-ways-you-can-be-a-better-help-meet-fd7a8226b9d2.

Wellman, Jack. 2014. "Different Types of Love Found in the Bible." *The Christian Post.* June 19. http://blogs.christianpost.com/better-than-i-deserve/different-types-of-love-found-in-the-bible-21799/.

Whitmore, Susan. 2012. "Are You Having an Identity Crisis?" *Psychology Today.* March 3. www.psychologytoday.com/us/blog/fulfillment-any-age/201203/are-you-having-identity-crisis.

About the Author

Dwight DeRamus's avocation is serving others through hearts, minds, and souls with the absolute truth by teaching and speaking from the Word of God through Jesus Christ. His vocation is in the field of education, where he has taught at high school and college levels for over 15 years in the Chicagoland area. Dwight is the author of three books, including the 2019 Human Relations Indie Book Award winner *Disappearing Dads*, he and is a contributing author to *BLISS for Singles* online magazine.

He has a passion to communicate God's design for the family. With that purpose in mind, Dwight seeks to provide everyone the tools and resources they need to deepen spiritually, strengthen their marriage and relationships with their children, and encourage young people to make sound decisions to take their lives in a new direction God has intended. Dwight has also presented multiple workshops and participated in discussion panels with a variety of audiences. He also serves as a deacon and Sunday school superintendent at his church. Dwight enjoys spending time with his family, working out, watching college and professional sports, and listening to jazz and old-school R&B music. Dwight DeRamus lives in the Chicagoland area serving as a husband for over twenty-six years and is a proud father of two sons. Go to www.treynickelpub.com for more information.

www.ingramcontent.com/pod-product-compliance
Lightning Source LLC
Chambersburg PA
CBHW020547030426
42337CB00013B/993